Suddenly Single:
A Life After Death

SHIRES ● PRESS

4869 Main Street

P.O. Box 2200

Manchester Center, VT 05255 www.northshire.com

Suddenly Single: A Life After Death Miriam S. Russell

©2017 by Miriam S. Russell ISBN: 978-1-60571-348-9

Building Community, One Book at a Time

A family-owned, independent bookstore in

Manchester Ctr., VT, since 1976 and Saratoga Springs, NY since 2013.

We are committed to excellence in bookselling.

The Northshire Bookstore's mission is to serve as a resource for
information, ideas, and entertainment while honoring the needs of
customers, staff, and community.

Printed in the United States of America

Suddenly Single:
A Life After Death

To Deb :

You are still my idol !
Thanks for all your
support.
Fondly,
Miriam

Miriam S. Russell

*To Bobbi Damp, without whose encouragement
and astute advice this book
would not have been possible.*

Chapter I

Sudden Death

This is the hour of lead
Remembered if outlived,
As freezing persons recollect the snow —
First chill, then stupor, then the letting go.

Emily Dickinson

The Last Time

The last time we left the opera, the fountain at Lincoln Center greeted us again, its silvery shards striving into the black sky.

He said, "That's where I want my ashes scattered."

"You always say that!" I replied with a wifely guffaw, "You aren't condemned to death like the tenor we just saw in *Andrea Chenier.*"

Earlier, my husband had rushed back from the box office with our tickets. "This must be a mistake," he said. "I ordered tickets in the Dress Circle balcony. These seats are in the front row of the orchestra." Taking advantage of the favorable blunder, we traipsed down the aisle and took our seats, expecting to be ousted any minute.

Our trip to New York City and the Metropolitan Opera that weekend was a celebration of Jim's retirement after 17 demanding years as the principal of four elementary schools in the Adirondack Mountains. To realize his retirement dream, we moved south to Virginia's Eastern Shore where the winters were more benign. Five years younger than Jim, I was not yet ready to retire. I took a fulltime job in the public schools while he was happy working part-time at the local community college. In our new home, he enjoyed listening to his extensive collection of classical music and opera recordings, puttering with his furniture refinishing projects and watching the ospreys on their big nests in the harbor. Then it happened.

1

It was an ordinary Friday in January–a month when the tomato and soybean fields lie fallow, waiting for an early spring. Instead of going directly home at the end of the school day, I drove in the opposite direction to buy fish fillets for supper. When I arrived home after four o'clock, everything was quiet.

"I'm home!" Silence answered. No music playing. No stirring at all.

Instead of looking in all the rooms, I went upstairs to change my shoes, thinking I would find Jim if I walked around the block. He had been walking regularly after he quit smoking a decade earlier on doctor's orders. Where was he? I expected to see his easy-going form sauntering along with his walking stick, a shillelagh he found years before. He was nowhere on our block. Circling back, I met one of my new neighbors, Gay Pindar, near the front walk and happily invited her in for tea. "I'm looking for my husband, but can't find him. He should be along later. Come on in and see our new place," I said. Ebullient as ever, Gay agreed and followed me inside.

Leading her onto the front porch I showed her into our sunny living-dining room. The large upper-story window under the cathedral ceiling illuminated the recently painted yellow walls. A new pastel overstuffed loveseat and chairs along with a soft green and pinkbraided rug completed my idea of southern living. I led Gay to our efficient new kitchen, which was such an improvement over our old one. At that moment, my pleasure was unburdened by ignorance. I had no idea that my new dream house contained the cataclysmic event of my life.

In the small den at the rear of the house —"*Oh God, no!*"—Jim was lying face down on the floor next to the desk—felled like a tree, legs and knees straight. His glasses lay beside his motionless head, slightly askew.We turned him over. "Oh, dear!" Gay said.

His face had dark bruises—no breath, no movement, but he was warm. "Honey, Honey!" I yelled as I shook his shoulders. We both tried mouth-to-mouth resuscitation with no response. Gay jumped up to call 911 while I pushed desperately on his chest. I looked at his open eyes—his sweet light brown eyes—now unresponsive, uncomprehending, devoid of life—futile to revive. He was gone—dead at 60. "Honey, Jim! Honey, Honey!" I started to cry.

Gay made more calls, and the house began to fill with emergency workers who soon left because there was no longer a life to save. They were replaced by friends and neighbors. When the coroner arrived, I left the den, trying to get away from the truth of what happened. Later someone suggested I go back into the room to be alone with Jim before they took him away. I knelt on the floor beside him, trying to grasp what had happened. He was there, but gone. A cruel, evil intruder had come into the house and snuffed him out. I felt his face and his hands, and kissed them. They were still warm. Then I fled the room, still crying, knowing that warmth was leaving his body.

After they took Jim's body away, I returned to the den, looking for clues, something that might have revealed what happened in those moments before he fell, but nothing was amiss. We had recently moved into the house, but things were pretty much in order, especially because he was always neat. The bathroom held no clues either, but in the kitchen, I could see the remains of his lunch in the sink—a few baked beans he rinsed off his plate, a lunch he favored when he was on his own.

During my crying and panic, someone called my mother. Matt, our journalist son, was still living in the Adirondacks. Outside it was cold and snowy. He was headed out to get a drink that Friday night when mother called him to tell him his father died.

She said, "It's your father."

From her tone, he guessed it. "Dad's dead."

"Yes."

When Matt called me, I was medicated, but tried to explain what happened,

"He landed right on his nose," I cried.

Christopher had been expecting his father to help him build some bookshelves in his apartment in D.C. He was at work in his classroom when the call came. He put the phone down and left the building immediately, explaining nothing, unable to articulate what he just heard. He had been expecting his Dad to come to him that weekend to help him install some shelves in his little apartment. Now he was traveling to the Eastern Shore to be with me as we prepared for his Dad's funeral service.

4

The neighbors came to the house and gathered around me, sitting an impromptu shiva. I met them with wet, red eyes. "I'm still crying!" Other friends were called. They found me shaking. Even though the pharmacy was closed for the evening, they made calls and shortly produced Xanax. Soon I was calmer and people started leaving. The last one said, "You shouldn't be alone," I heard myself reply, "I want to be alone so I can talk to Jim."

Before the memorial services, desperate for an explanation, some clue about what happened, I called Jim's doctor, thinking his death might have been related to a recent hernia repair.

"No," the doctor demurred, "A hernia-repair operation eight weeks ago, couldn't be linked to his death."

"Why did he die?" I asked.

"Sudden death" was his only explanation.

I'm an intelligent woman, and you are telling me that's it? The reason he died? There must be another explanation. There must be a "why." "Sudden death" is so inexplicable, such scanty cause to drop dead in your tracks, to stop breathing, to leave, to die and abandon life in an instant. You were his doctor, you treated him just recently, recommended him for a hernia repair. That's all you have? Sudden death?

There was no mention of an autopsy because in Virginia, they are performed only when there is suspicion of foul play. Later I learned I could have insisted on an autopsy. Why didn't I? I just wanted him back. I wanted

5

to hear him whistle his fancy melodies. I wanted to see him reading the paper, doing the crossword, tying his tie while he shifted his weight standing in front of the mirror. Yes, now I would like to know if it was a cerebral hemorrhage or a ruptured artery that felled him. It might be important for his sons to have that information, but at the time, my mind was stuck on my sudden loss, realizing, as Johnny Cash sang, "Sooner or later, God will strike you down."

Our new neighbors quickly arranged rides to pick up all my traveling friends and family members. True to southern hospitality, they provided each friend and family member was a bedroom for the night. They also graciously produced a steady stream of food at my home. The ham and biscuits, salads, cookies, cakes, and snacks were all eaten. The fillets for two I purchased from the fish market that fatal day were wrapped and frozen, to be found weeks later, a frozen reminder of how little we can prepare for life's events.

Premonitions

Thinking back, Jim seemed to have premonitions of his early demise for quite some time. When we first fell in love, he said, "Let's get married; I'm only going to live another 20 years or so." He was only 31 at the time, but perhaps his unusual proposal stemmed from early near-misses with death. At seven, he almost died of Bright's disease, and as a boy climbing on an iron picket fence, he fell, barely missing his genitals. Maybe after those close encounters he began to expect he'd die early, but fortunately, he lived three more decades, dying one month before our 30th anniversary.

In the midst of his 60th family birthday party, he stopped the conversation by announcing, "I never expected to make it this far." Why would he not expect to live a long healthy life? Other than a chronic back problem, he was healthy. Later, I was shocked to find a three-by-five card in his desk titled, "Health Insurance." In the middle of the card was the cryptic message: *Miriam is covered when I die. Notify SL School District.* It seems he not only expected to leave, but made sure my health care would be provided for when he did.

Jim fit a lot of significant events into his last month. It tore my heart to hear from friends at a distance who had recently received a Christmas note from him.

"I'm retired and life is sweet," he wrote to everyone.

The furniture refinishing projects were finished. The lovely beechwood side table fit perfectly in our den, and an old hardwood maple chest of drawers now gleamed in our bedroom. His model boats and ships were finished except for the sails on one. There was no evidence he was going to pick up another modeling project, but he had enrolled in a watercolor class, working carefully to create sketches and scenes featuring small boats on the nearby waterfront. One of my friends who was in class with him said, "he kept us in stitches" with his quips and self-deprecating remarks about his own painting skills. I found his canvases neatly packed away in a closet. When his art instructor, Thelma Jarvis Peterson, was having a gallery show in Virginia Beach, we bought her framed plate magnolia watercolor. Now it hangs prettily on my living room wall where I can admire it, remembering the excitement Jim and I shared in acquiring it.

Several weeks before he died, Jim traveled to the Yucatan with an older friend who was in failing health, leading us to wonder if this might be the last time they would be together. Larry Mowers was a Harvard musicologist who introduced Jim to classical music and guided his musical tastes as a young student in Ithaca.

Their friendship was sustained over the years by Larry's old-fashioned letters brimming with self-effacing wit.

While they were away, I was alarmed by a report in the news of a Mexican tourist bus accident. I called the hotel in Merida where they were supposed to be. They hadn't checked in yet. After leaving a frantic message, I spent an anxious day and a half before Jim returned my call.

"Are you OK? There was a tourist bus accident. People were injured. One person died." I blathered, annoyed he hadn't called earlier.

"We're fine; didn't hear of an accident, just spent the day at the pyramids at Chichen Itza."

"OK, but I was frantic. I called the tour office to find where you would be staying. Geez, I'm glad you called back."

The connection faded, shortening the call. Saying goodbye, his voice seemed to disappear into space: "I love you..."

He returned late at night. Dopey with sleep, I acted like an annoyed parent whose teenage child had stayed out too late, but his embrace soothed my pique.

Too soon, he had to go out of town again to a conference related to his job. I'd heard about that part time position at the Eastern Shore Community College and thought it would be a perfect match for him. Apparently the search committee agreed with my assessment, since they decided to keep him in the interview room until he said "yes."

Looking back, maybe I should not have encouraged him to take that job. He was reluctant to go to an overnight conference, complaining of tiredness. The day he came back, he went to bed with a pain in the right side of his neck. I rubbed his neck and ran my fingers through his steel gray curls and he slept. The next morning, I found him sleeping on the couch in the den, something he had never done before. By the time I dressed myself, he was up and moving around. Without a perfunctory kiss goodbye, I hurried off to work, not knowing it would be the last time I would see him alive.

Memorials

How to start a new life after sudden death? The curtain had come down abruptly on my identity as a wife. I wondered how I could cope, but my mind was clouded and emotions wanted to dominate. Planning two Memorial services seemed to help.

For the first service in Virginia, Jim's picture rested on the table in the front of the church along with his ashes in a latch-less mahogany box. Jim, who was my husband, had now become ashes. Mother and I were alone in the house, grabbing a quick lunch prior to the first memorial service. I couldn't eat and began to tear up. "Your bladder's near your eyes," she said. Seeing my tears, mother recalled her sad childhood and her father's abuse. I know she was trying to show me that she didn't cry about her miserable experiences; therefore, neither should I. How could she be so insensitive in choosing this time to tell me of the worst times in her life? Somehow, her model of stoicism seemed to help me, since I sat dryeyed throughout the two ceremonies.

The memorial service programs magically appeared, listing selections of recorded music and Jim loved best including his favorite hymn by Gottschalk,

> *Soon from us the light of day*
> *Shall forever pass away;*
> *Then, from sin and sorrow free,*
> *Take us, Lord, to dwell with thee.*

Jim was an enthusiastic collector of everything Gottschalk wrote: his scores, his biography and piano renditions of his compositions. When he learned Gottschalk was buried in Brooklyn, he found the grave and took a picture of the tombstone.

The service included a recording of his Elementary school's choir singing Beethoven's *Ode to Joy* that I found in his cassette collection. At the end of the much-too-short recording, he was heard speaking as the school's principal, thanking the children for their song and urging applause.

Hearing his voice during the ceremony was hard to bear. How I wished he had said more.

For the second memorial service at the First Presbyterian Church in Saranac Lake where we had been members before his retirement, I asked three of his closest friends to speak. Fellow retired principal in Lake Placid Al Macnab's eulogy took the form of a letter of recommendation to St. Peter.

> *Dear Rev. Simon Peter:*
>
> *Please accept this letter of recommendation and reference for Mr. James R. Russell who we understand has entered your employ on 22 January 1993.*
>
> *I have known Mr. Russell since August of 1973, both personally and professionally.*

We have worked together on numerous educational projects, projects which have succeeded primarily due to his enthusiasm and leadership. Mr. Russell is a unique individual. He is first and foremost a Christian and one who believes deeply in family values. This is a man who has always been highly respected by his friends and colleagues for his advice in times of trouble as he will always be willing to listen. In brief, St. Peter, you are going to find this man a joy to work with. He has numerous talents which I know you will find useful in the Resurrection, but there are three that I would like to bring to your attention.

First, as mentioned, Mr. Russell is a "people person" as you no doubt have already found out. You may wish to place him back in teaching as he is one of the best in the business. Students at all levels respond well to his warm but firm approach and his relaxed attitude.

Another possibility you may also consider Mr. Russell for is something in the field of music.

I have met few people who have a more avid or passionate interest in the great oratorios and operas. I thought perhaps if Puccini or Mozart were working on a new piece, Mr. Russell could be assigned to work with them as their rehearsal soloist. You will be impressed with his voice (if you haven't been already). In any event, he should without question, become immediately assigned to your senior choir.

Mr. Russell, in addition to the above, is a carpenter of sorts, an interest generated by watching the TV series, "This Old House." Although not what I would call a Master Builder, he could be used for odd jobs where needed.

If these positions are presently filled, I might suggest that he be assigned as a supervisor on such jobs. Mr. Russell greatly enjoys supervising anything and everything and has great skill in this area.

I can assure you, this is a man who will become of great value to you. He does not drink to excess (well, hardly ever). There was that evening at the Belvedere and of course the night on Upper Saranac, but you know about those already. He has always been kind and thoughtful to his family, friends and colleagues. For these reasons and others, I recommend Mr. James R. Russell to you without reservation.

Very truly yours,
Alan D. Macnab

P.S. St. Peter, you have yourself a damn good man.

I saved William Carrozzo's tribute as well:

Jim and I have been friends for almost forty years. Our friendship was formed in college, we had classes together, played intramural sports and were fortunate to act together in several college productions. We even toured for the college in an excerpt show of "Carousel" trying to drum up ticket sales.

Like most people, we drifted apart after college, but always managed to stay in touch and when Jim started working in Westchester County and I in New York, we took up where we left off.

When we weren't on my old boat, we were making excursions in his Buick convertible that should have been retired a decade before. Our friendship was nurtured in those years.

Those were excellent times, touch football in the Sheep Meadow in Central Park, driving to Coney Island at 3 am for a hot dog at Nathan's, Atlantic Beach, Jones Beach. I had an old cabin cruiser at the time and one of our favorite outings was to leave Flushing Bay and make our way up the East River and out

14

to the Hudson, then we would cruise down the Hudson past all the great ocean liners and wish them "bon voyage" as we continued down to the tip of Manhattan and then make our way back to our mooring. Jim was always a little leery of my credibility as a boat captain, especially when it came to putting the boat into the slip. He would place himself forward, armed with a boat hook and give me one, most unnautical dramatic direction in Italian –"PIANO-PIANO!"

I think our friendship solidified after Jim and Miriam were married. Then we didn't see each other as much, but we still stayed in touch.

Our friendship had taken on an easy sort of, "Stay in touch; I'm here if you need me; visit when you can." That was the relationship and it never wavered.

He was a true and honest friend, and I, we, are better for having known him."

William Carrozzo

Jim's pal and fellow Saranac Lake Principal, Warner Houth, also spoke. He said, "Of all the times in my life, those I spent with Jim were the most fun."

The morning after the second February memorial service was especially clear and cold as I bid dear friends Bob and Bobbi Damp goodbye. Jim always drove, but now, numb and alone, I was in the driver's seat. On my way out of town, I stopped to watch the mid-winter construction of the Ice Palace by Lake Flower in the middle of town. Marlene, my hairdresser, and community volunteer, hailed me from atop the ice blocks. "How are you?" she shouted. "I don't think I know yet." I waved back. "That's OK," she returned.

Driving myself out of the mountains through the Cascades, and down the valley south to the flat Eastern Shore, I faced great uncertainty, but with one ambition, to continue working full time and compose my new life as a single woman.

Remaining Remains

Although the idea of carrying remains with me was repellant, somehow, I had to obey Jim's last wish to have his ashes scattered in that fountain in New York's Lincoln Center. I sent invitations to our closest friends to meet me at the fountain in front of the Met on the Saturday after Thanksgiving. The deed would be done. Still, how could I actually transport his cremains in such a big mahogany box? It seemed an overwhelming problem until a friend offered to ask the funeral home to put some of the ashes in a paper bag; he would carry it with him to New York City and Lincoln Center.

I dreaded the thought of scattering ashes because I was told that it's not like the movies where they float and shimmer in the wind before dropping into the earth or water. The remains can be in pieces; bone fragments can be discerned, and there is no guarantee of a cosmic moment. I wanted no part of opening that box myself, for fear of having to look at the contents.

Under cover of darkness, we gathered by the noisy fountain, wondering how to actually *put the stuff in there* over the two-foot ledge. Christopher agreed to climb up on the flat ledge and drop the contents into the water.

Forming a phalanx around him, we tried to conceal our activity from the watchful guard standing nearby. Roz Rees says she saw the guard move back and out of the way after Gregg Smith quietly explained to him that we were going to have a brief ceremony there. Joanne Decker, newly ordained in a New Age sect, recited some inspirational words as the ashes fell. Together, we sang the Doxology, holding hands around part of the fountain – still striving into the dark as it had the last night Jim and I saw it together. Furtively giggling at our success, we crossed Broadway to a restaurant where we had a few drinks and shared favorite stories about Jim.

Everyone remembered how each evening at five o'clock, the school Principal would settle in his easy chair with a Manhattan cocktail. They joked that the neighbors could tell what time it was from the clinking of ice in his glass. Another remembered during the opera season, he could be found in the den, listening to the Met matinee performance on the FM radio while watching a football game, preferably the Giants, with the television sound turned off so he could enjoy his two great passions simultaneously.

Back home after our Lincoln Center escapade, the big heavy box with the remaining remains was waiting for me. The funeral director explained there was a lot more in the box than could have been easily carried in a brown paper lunch bag.

Most of his ashes were still in there. Still determined to fulfill Jim's wishes, I turned to another water idea. Knowing how much Jim loved watching the ospreys in the harbor, it seemed an appropriate place to scatter the remaining remains. I prevailed on friends who had an outboard motor boat. We put the mahogany box in a crab trap weighted with bricks, planning to drop it into the water from their outboard motor boat. One summer evening when Chris was visiting from DC, we stopped in the middle of the quiet harbor for the final send-off. I softly sang the verse of *On Eagle's Wings,* the song based on the 91st psalm:

> *And He will raise you up on eagle's wings,*
> *Bear you on the breath of dawn,*
> *Make you to shine like the sun,*
> *And hold you in the palm of His Hand*

Tears began as I choked up on the last verse, watching as the dark mahogany box in the crab cage slid into the water, but instead of sinking, it floated away.

We watched it go towards the nearby shore as one friend quipped, "He must know it's Manhattan time."

"It can't float over to the shore to have someone else find it there." Yelling and laughing now, we retrieved it back in the boat. Giving up, I grimly brought the box home and put it unceremoniously on a closet shelf. It was fortunate our plan failed because later we learned in most coastal areas of the US, cremated ashes are required to be scattered three miles or more from shore.

According to *Feng Shui for Dummies*, the auspicious arrangement of the environment and home décor insures health and happiness; but also, there is a particular admonition against keeping belongings of the deceased around. The widow is not supposed to find anyone else to love if memorabilia and photos of the deceased are in the room with her. I'm sure that includes keeping cremains in one's bedroom closet too. If true, it's fine with me, because Jim Russell was a most unique guy; no one could come close to replacing him.

Along with his positive enthusiasm for life, his unique sense of humor made him irresistible. He entertained me again when I was going through his papers. I found a quote from Princess Ida, one of Gilbert and *Sullivan's witty operettas:*

> *Oh! Don't the days seem lank and long,*
> *When everything's right and nothing goes wrong?*
> *And isn't your life extremely flat*

When I moved again, I placed the mahogany box in my new bedroom closet shelf along with Jim's precious opera books, and his collection of Opera recordings. There they would stay until I could decide where we are both going to end up together. Feng Shui be dammed; at least it was something to grumble at.

Grief and Coping

It is true, as Jung observed, "it is in the subconscious that the living coexist with the dead."

My dreams were of being lost in dark hallways, then finding crowds of busy people walking in and out of rooms. Official-looking people with nametags spoke to each other as they passed. I tried to interrupt, clinging to myself, arms folded on my chest. "Please help me, I cried tearfully. I lost my bag with $200 and I can't find my jacket or my suitcase. Please help me."

Most difficult were my dream reunions with Jim.

He would appear and I'd tell him I was so glad to see him and we'd try to cook a meal together, but it was like trying to push through mud to fully know what was happening before waking up to cruel disappointment. There is probably nothing more disheartening than to wake and realize the reunion was only oneiric.

After weeks of free floating anxiety, I turned to my minister for some counseling. She sat across from me in my living room and we talked. Her sympathetic voice challenged, "Do you have any regrets?"

"No, no regrets," I lied.

She invited me to pray with her, and I readily agreed, but soon convulsed into hysterical tears, gasping for breath. Alarmed, she suggested I breathe into a paper bag. With the bag over my nose and mouth, the mood changed; I felt a bit comical and could relax.

"That was real fear," she opined.

With anxiety mounting, I continued to take Xanax. Soon after, I stayed home from work, feeling peculiarly ill at ease, and shaky; perhaps I had returned to the job too soon after what happened. It was strange to have trouble concentrating, feeling as Joyce Carol Oates wrote, "like an ambulatory assemblage of symptoms like a skeleton rattling about in a loose gunny sack." In case my condition was caused by the Xanax, I threw out the pills, stopping them cold-turkey, not realizing doing so made the problem worse.

The withdrawal symptoms added to my typical textbook reaction to sudden death, defined as "the manifestation of an agitation, a flight or flee response to a perceived threat." I was slipping into an agitated depression, a day-to-day panic leaving me limp, yet anxious.

A friend connected me with his daughter, a physician who treats addiction. She prescribed a tapering off regime for the Xanax and the shakiness began to dissipate.

Starting regular counseling sessions at the local mental health center, I owned up to some painful regrets. I missed the chance to have lunch with Jim the day he died. Driving to one of my assigned schools near our house when I saw his new blue and white truck, turning into our road. My destination was the school, only a block away from our road. At the time, I remember thinking, "I could follow him home and we could have lunch together," but I didn't. It would have been out of character for me to skip out of work in the middle of the day when school would be dismissed in a couple of hours anyway.

In the same vein, I regretted going up the highway to the fish store before driving home. I hadn't been there when he came in from his walk, or I might have heard him fall in the den. I'll never know the answers, but those days, I was haunted by those questions, drifting, trying to find a way forward on my own.

Lost Memories

Sudden death meant there were no opportunities for goodbyes, no memorial service plans, nor expressions of love or anticipated loss—no admonitions regarding how he would feel about my remarrying. All those things we fantasize we would say and do if we knew our time was near. If Jim had been suffering a long illness, or in if I had a fatal illness, would we have indulged in those expressions? Instead of giving in to the inevitable, would we have concentrated on the next best treatment, the next possible surcease from pain?

There is some comfort in the knowledge that given a choice, Jim would have preferred a sudden death. It's almost impossible to imagine him with a lingering sickness and slowly diminishing faculties. Having lived a bit longer than he had expected, he enjoyed life fully and overall, quite happily.

One of those happy times was his 60th birthday party at mother's house with all the family gathered. We were laughing about the ugly decorations I created with a squeeze tube on the sheet cake I baked. The frosting stuck as it came of the tube–the results were, "Happ irthd y." Again, we heard Jim say, without apparent cause, "I never expected to live this long." I took a video of the fun to enjoy later.

While we were cleaning up, Jim took the video camera with him on a furtive excursion to Wendy's for a hamburger with Matt and the cousins. Unknown to him, the camera was rolling in his lap, directed up at his face while he warned everyone, "Don't tell Miriam" about where they had been, assuming I would disapprove of eating fast food hamburgers.

It was a wonderful surprise to find that scene among our video tapes the next spring. I intended to keep that precious video as a symbol—a means of keeping him vivid. It was all done in good humor and I looked forward to watching it often when I was alone.

During the ensuing weeks, I also recorded the television program, *Northern Lights*, a program Jim and I had enjoyed together. When I told our dear friend Grace Stay, whom Jim loved as the daughter he never had, about the funny video from Jim's birthday party, she asked to see it and took it home. After watching it all the way through from beginning to the end, she returned it, telling me it was the wrong video because there was nothing on it but episodes of "Northern Lights."

Panic mounted as I looked for the right video, but never found it because I had recorded over it and obliterated this precious memory. This was another loss; the symbolic comfort I expected from it was gone. I mourned again. It had been a bonus, a piece of cake to be saved and savored later; now I felt bitterness and hurt, chastising myself for my carelessness.

In her memoir, *A Year of Magical Thinking*, Joan Didion needed to save her husband's shoes after his death, magically thinking he would need them. In contrast, I had no difficulty giving away Jim's clothing or tools because they went to his sons. Matt and Chris wore some of his Pendleton wool shirts for years afterward and they were happy to have their Dad's tools. A wall of LP albums, cassettes, shelves of books and CDs carefully collected over the years was left. It was several years before I could listen to them by myself.

Most are still with me. Every time I try to sort through them for disposal, I decide to wait. When I do play them, my connection with him feels strong. How I wish we had time left to share them together; before, I often busied myself with something else instead of giving his music my undivided attention.

Jim's contagious enthusiasm for opera was major part of what we had shared together, but I still can't bear to hear the strains of his favorite, Puccini's *La Boheme*. It's an emotional arrow and I avoid it.

Now when I'm in the audience enjoying other Puccini operas, I hear his voice explaining the characteristics of the long melody lines. Remembering his lessons, I consider myself lucky to have had his musical legacy growing in me throughout our marriage. The seedlings were already there, since I already valued classical music before we met. As a young girl assigned to clean her room on Saturdays, I heard the Texaco Metropolitan Opera broadcasts during the winter seasons.

Rise Stevens became my idol after hearing her sing Carmen for the first time.

Shortly after Jim passed away, I remembered he had purchased tickets for a Verdi Requiem performance with the Virginia Beach Symphony.

"Passed away." *Should I use that euphemism? It doesn't change things. Why does that phrase repel me? He died, darn it, let's face the bitter truth. Passing away sounds so mild. Death isn't mild, it's catastrophic. Why deny it? Do we feel better to just think of it as "passing away?"*

I invited Grace to use Jim's ticket to go with me to the Verdi performance in Virginia Beach as a private musical memorial. Twelve years later, I sang the alto part in that same divinely inspired piece with the Masterworks Chorus in Albany. Later, I had the chance to sing it once more in the huge amphitheater at Chautauqua. Singing there, with 100 other voices was another peak experience; the joy of the Agnus Dei when the kettle drum sounds the terrifying introduction, vibrates bones and shivers the spine, the ending—libera me—*"free me, oh free me from eternal death"* is other-worldly. Thank you for the tickets, Jim.

Messages

The phone—the sound of his voice on the answering machine—a precious sound, but so heartbreakingly misleading. Knowing of his death, would callers be rattled by hearing Jim's voice? I had to change his message, so I recorded my own. When I heard voice messages, I had no urge to return the call. Disembodied voices, people who heard the news called my name—voices dripping with horror and pity. I let them go, unable to extend myself by sharing their shock.

However, some calls from family and friends were easy to return. They listened without pity, their voices full of assurance—I would be all right. Favoring some friends over others seems capricious, something ungracious, a lack of character, like failing to send thankyou note for sympathy cards, foodstuffs, plants, or offers of help. My focus was to just get through each day at work.

Another disturbing message came regularly, a male voice I did not know—a strange ominous message I did not want. Consequently, Matt recorded a generic message for me; one that would not give away the truth that here lives a woman on her own, vulnerable to prey from strangers. This widow did not want to return calls, certainly not calls left by a strange male voice.

Crying Through the Nineties

I had been spared the agony of loss by death until Dad died in 1991. In our family, death had been elsewhere, but it arrived then, a year and a month before Jim's passing. After Dad's funeral service, hiding from the rest of my dry-eyed family, I ran into the bathroom to have a few "boo-hoos" by myself before the trip to the cemetery, After a minute, my sister-in-law knocked on the door and scurried me outside where the hearse and funeral procession was waiting. No time for tears.

When Mother died in 1999, I didn't cry until she was laid out in the funeral home. She looked about fourteen years old, wearing a pink dress we had to buy for her because she was so thin from not eating for over a year except through a feeding tube. At 86, her skin was smooth and her hair was combed down on her forehead with youthful bangs. I was carrying on loudly when my nieces walked in and I sobered up. I already learned that my family, like my mother, had no truck with tears.

The first year I faced Thanksgiving dinner as a widow was hard on the rest of the family because of me. Everyone held hands in a large circle for the grace, which Matt delivered so beautifully in remembrance of his father and his grandfather. I started to tear up, then tried to stop, but in the trying, sobs overcame me. I must have upset everyone greatly because they've never remembered Jim or Dad again in a Thanksgiving grace. However, I do, silently, on my own without tears.

The 90's are over and with it my crying, for as George Burns observed, "You cry and you cry and then there are no more tears."

Equilibrium

It was hard to find my equilibrium at times, especially when it involved minor legal infractions. About a year after Jim's death, I sailed through a small town outside of my own neighborhood, doing about 40 mph. A cop stopped me for exceeding the town speed limit and asked for my license and registration.

"Get out of the car. You can't drive until you get your license renewed. It expired last year."

"Um, how will I get home?"

"Get a ride. And leave the car here." He repeated, "You can't drive your car without a valid license."

I called Gay, but she wasn't home. I called another neighbor, my voice wavering a bit, "I'm in a spot; my license expired and I can't drive my car home." She chuckled, and agreed to come for me. It's humiliating when you are going through difficulty of your own making and it amuses others. Maybe they don't want to make you feel worse by showing sympathy, so they laugh at your predicament. In my mood, I brooked neither sympathy nor giggles. Now I enjoy telling stories of my mishaps, misjudgments and miscalculations, but I was touchy as a mousetrap then.

There is no dearth of advice for widows and widowers: "Get a Grip on Finances," "Eat meals in a different place," "Make your home your own," and "Assume Control." They should also include "Remember to renew your driver's license" because death seems to bring irresponsibility, and causes slip-ups in unexpected ways.

When it was time to see the judge, my nerves were tingling, wondering what I would say. He looked at the policeman's charge, then at me, "Driving without a license?" His voice had an incredulous tone.

Playing the widow card, I explained, "I had a license – been driving with one for over 40 years, but last year, my husband died and I forgot to renew it."

"Mrs. Russell, pay the clerk $15. Next!"

Was he a really nice judge, or was becoming widow a good excuse for negligence?

It was still hard to be a completely responsible person a few years later while starting a new consulting business. I was living in a small apartment near Mother's nursing home in Saratoga County while waiting for my house on the shore to sell. One evening, I found a client's check for $64 and absentmindedly threw the envelope with the check in the trash. After dark, I realized I had pitched it with the trash into the parking lot dumpster. Armed with a flashlight and a step-stool, I climbed up and jumped into the dumpster to retrieve the bag with the check. Luckily, the dumpster wasn't too deep and I climbed out, with the check in hand. It was time for a mini-celebration, and after cleaning up a bit, I drove to the nearest ice cream store to treat myself to a chocolate chip cone.

I was driving slowly toward home while licking the ice cream in the dark when a police car suddenly appeared behind me, lights flashing like the fourth of July. When the officer approached, he couldn't ignore the dripping cone in my hand. "Oh, you have a cone," he said, but ticketed me for rolling through a stop sign. The ticket cost $84, wiping out amount of the newly-found check. Obviously, I was neglecting life's ordinary requirements.

Social Security Disbursement

One of my duties as a new widow was to take myself to the local Social Security Office to collect a "One Time Widow's Benefit." Expecting sympathy, I approached the clerk.

"My husband died last month. Here's his death certificate." I blurted, "He was only 60."

Indifferently, she asked, "Then he wasn't collecting Social Security benefits?"

"No."

Evidently women with deceased husbands were a routine matter around here.

"How long were you married?"

"Well, our 30th wedding anniversary would have been next month."

Pressure inside me forced up through my throat — *Must not break down, must not cry. Stay in control.*

"How many times was he married?"

"Once before."

"How long was he married before? Less than 10 years?"

"Yes, less than 10 years."

"If they were married for more than 10 years, his first wife would be eligible for a widow's benefit."

I felt diminished. *Oh God, why is she telling me about this? He was my husband, no others. It was so long ago; they divorced before we met.*

"How many times have you been married?"

"Once before."

"Were you married more than 10 years?"

"A little over a year, Why?"

The tight pressure in my throat was harder to hold down now.

"In cases of divorce, if your former spouse dies before you do and your marriage lasted at least ten years, you can collect benefits in the same manner as if you were still married at the time of death."

I was sorry I asked and my head swam with resentment.

What was this? I'm a widow whose only husband of almost 30 years died suddenly at only 60 and left me forever. My early unhappy marriage was a mistake. It happened to another person, a person I am no longer. My identity has changed completely. I was Jim Russell's wife and am now his widow. No other woman's loss. Please, why all these questions? Just let me sign something and get out of here.

"How long did the deceased work?"

"Since college—over 40 years, I guess. He retired a little over three years ago. He was still working part time."

Geez, this is horrible; you are horrible. We're talking about someone who worked hard all his life, he finally retired, just started enjoying his retirement, getting away from the stress. We just moved into our dream house; he was a father and my husband! Let's not call him the "deceased." He had a name; people knew him and loved him; I loved him and I found cut down like a tree—his legs didn't bend—he was face down on the floor—still warm, but gone—I hate that word—"deceased."

I struggled for self-control as she kept bombarding me with her bureaucratic expertise:

"Social Security pays $255 as a one-time payment upon death, if the decedent worked long enough. This payment does not repeat and does not affect any other Social Security benefits you may receive."

That was it for the widow's disbursement—$255 dollars? All the time and all those Social Security contributions—he worked—he contributed, and it ended worth $255 dollars? I give up.

I have other resources—the widow, somehow, will survive. Born in May, my horoscope says, "People born under the Gemini sign have the ability to discard the past and look quickly ahead to the unpredictable future while playing their own role in the present." I had to believe that description.

Chapter II

Reflections

*A longing to inquire
Into the mystery of this hear which
beats So wild, so deeply in us — to
know Whence our lives come and
where they go.*

Matthew Arnold

Meeting Jim

We met at a conference of speech language therapists in 1962, held in the Hotel Pennsylvania in New York City. I was in the hotel pharmacy buying a razor to shave my legs. At the register, I noticed two fellows watching my purchase behind me. "Excuse me," one said, "Are you going to shave, or slit your throat?"

I blushed with embarrassment, grabbed my purchase, and left. Later in the lobby, I ran into them again and the same fellow stopped me, "Pardon me, but the button in the back of your blouse is undone!" Reaching behind my neck to slip the button in place, I stopped and took a good look at both. The brash questioner was smiling, but the taller one looked more serious. I was struck by his brown spaniel eyes and his high forehead surrounded by a mane of curly dark hair. "Well," I said, "Am I talking to a couple of single guys?"

"I'm Joe," said the brash one, fingering his wedding ring "And I'm married."

"I'm divorced," said the taller one who looked like James Garner, "I'm Jim Russell."

"I'm Miriam and I'm getting divorced too." I said, looking again into those spaniel eyes. "Will you be at the dance in the ballroom tonight?" he asked. I thought I could see my future in his face. He had such a sweet smile, and those brown eyes captured my heart immediately. "Yes."

"See you there," he said. We would meet again; we would dance together. I was already in love.

Later, I felt like Cinderella arriving at the ball. But where was my Prince? One of my graduate school professors was at the entrance and I stopped to say hello. Then Jim appeared. As he strolled easily towards me, my spirit rose like a balloon and dropped just as quickly as he continued past me in the wide entrance and asked a woman standing behind me to dance. He danced with her the rest of the evening. The instant he passed by, my balloon popped. Stifling great disappointment, I danced with another guy the rest of the evening, wishing they were him.

Later, in a reckless mood, I stopped by a smaller hospitality party. It was crowded and the liquor was flowing. I picked up a gin and tonic and took a vacant seat next to a slight fellow on a couch, happy to see Jim was seated opposite. He watched as the inebriated guy sitting next to me leaned in close and offered to spend the night with me. Without thinking, I poured my drink on his head and he sputtered; I got up and walked quickly to the other side of the room.

Jim followed me, asking, "Do you want me to walk you out?"

"Yes, you may. Oh yes." My heart leapt joyfully as we found our way out of the hotel and walked up Broadway. "Why didn't you ask me to dance earlier?" I prodded.

"I thought you were with someone else."

"No, you saw me talking with my graduate school professor."

We walked for blocks, sharing our life stories. I was recovering from a short, unhappy marriage, and Jim had been divorced for a couple of years. He had a young son, Ed, who lived with his mother in California. "I love him," Jim told me, "And he knows I love him." Jim explained that he had been too young to be a father and he left. He admitted it was hard to talk about his young son, but could only see him for a few weeks in the summers.

I talked about extracting myself from an earlier marriage that had nothing to redeem it. I had gone to marriage counseling, but my spouse wouldn't. It soon became divorce counseling for me alone. I moved out. In twelve months, I was divorced.

We went to his room and talked some more. After sharing our stories and feeling the mounting mutual attraction, we didn't want to separate. We started out in two separate twin beds; then he turned out the light and asked me to come into his.

Coming from an unhappy short marriage, Jim seemed to be the one I sought, and the safety I needed. In the morning, he left to give a presentation at the conference and I returned to my own room to find a huge bouquet. How did Jim have time to arrange this? He hadn't. It was sent by the man I danced with the evening before.

It was the day before Thanksgiving and we were in Jim's car headed north on the Thruway. We were both spending the holiday with our families, mine in

Rensselaer, his to the west in Ithaca, considerably out of the way. Dad met us at the Albany exit and Jim jumped out of the car with me. I started introductions. "This is my Dad." Then I hesitated, suddenly unsure of Jim's last name.

He stepped in and proffered his hand. "Jim Russell, sir, nice to meet you."

During the next year, we spent each weekend together, driving back and forth on the parkways between his apartment in Yonkers and mine in West Hartford. On Sunday when we left each other, I felt bereft, impatient for the next time we could be together. I resigned my job in Connecticut and found a new job teaching English in a middle school in Mamaroneck, much closer to Jim in Yonkers.

When JFK was assassinated, we searched out a special memorial service, choosing to go to the one held in the Cathedral of St. John the Divine. We saw "Tom Jones" and "The Birds" at the movies, ate in Italian restaurants, and sang along with the libretto of *Der Fledermaus* while getting drunk on red wine celebrating the New Year of 1964 with Bill Carozzo and his girlfriend Rita.

Jim's enthusiasm for opera attracted invitations to lecture at local singles groups. He was a devoted Italophile, with pictures of Verdi, Brahms and Puccini on the wall and a large LP collection of complete operas. Despite some college and community theater singing roles under his belt, he confessed he would "give his right arm" to be able to sing better. "Done." I said. I knew of a voice coach in Manhattan who gave us both lessons. Although he had a tenor range, Jim was more comfortable in baritone roles. I can still faintly hear him practicing some of the long Puccini phrases in Gianni Schicchi or *"Che gelida manina"* from *La Boheme*.

We shared a special poem, *Dover Beach* by Matthew Arnold:

> *Ah, love, let us be true*
> *To one another! for the world, which seems*
> *To lie before us like a land of dreams,*
> *So various, so beautiful, so new,*
> *Hath really neither joy, nor love, nor light,*
> *Nor certitude, nor peace, nor help for pain;*
> *And we are here as on a darkling plain*
> *Swept with confused alarms of struggle and flight,*
> *Where ignorant armies clash by night.*

We formed our own little island, a bulwark against the hardships we both had suffered, a place where the future seemed like that new "land of dreams."

We would face our fates together in marriage. We traded my diamond ring from my early marriage for a new one while making plans for our wedding. My family was already captivated by Jim and Mother helped us with wedding plans. Should we have the reception catered? Anything elaborate for a second marriage for both of us would be unseemly in those days, but at least we could

41

have some catering. Knowing my sister was also divorced, Jim teased mother, "Go ahead, Ruth, your daughters get married only two or three times." Somehow, only Jim could make a remark like that sound charming.

Marriage, Birth and the New Feminism

When we were first married, we lived in a lovely prewar Tudor apartment house in Pelham Manor where we could take full advantage of being near the city.

Pregnant for most of that time, I'd fall asleep in the car before we left Manhattan after an opera at the Met or City Center. We were both taking voice lessons from Luigi Vellucci in the city and performed together locally in summer band concerts. Jim didn't want to rehearse, but I would wear out my voice with over-rehearsing. It bothered me that he used lyrics on a card instead of memorizing them; so, for the sake of marital harmony, we stopped our duo act.

I preferred singing solo rather than expecting Jim to conform to my standards of rehearsal. So he babysat while I, four months pregnant with Christopher, rehearsed the role of Pamina in Mozart's *Magic Flute* for a small church production. We joined the Lutheran church because Jim liked the music-filled services. Both of our sons were baptized there in New Rochelle.

Toward the end of the school year, my position was eliminated due to a precipitous drop in enrollment for the upcoming school year. When I applied at the unemployment office while noticeably pregnant, the clerk asked me if I was, and turned me away without unemployment benefits. That summer I called one of Jim's friends who was staffing a day camp and asked for a job there. "Well, you're pregnant now, and we don't want pregnant women around young children."

"What group of people would be more likely to be around pregnant women than young children?" I thought. A first-grade teacher I had worked with was pregnant, but she was replaced with only a month left in the school year. At the time, the policy was "five months pregnant, and you're out." Feeling sorry for the children's loss of an important relationship, I questioned the policy, speaking with the assistant superintendent about this unnecessary precaution. "If we let women teach in their late pregnancies, they'd be giving birth in the classrooms," he explained. The surge in feminism in the '60s started to open my eyes to those wrongful policies.

Our son Matthew was barely six months old when we were astounded to learn I was pregnant again. I found a tutoring job that required me to leave him in the apartment in the late afternoon before Jim got home. We hired the babysitter who also took care of Matt while we were singing in the choir on Sunday mornings. One afternoon, Jim came home a bit earlier than usual, and walked into the living room to find Matt still in his playpen with a wet diaper. The babysitter came out of our bedroom followed by two boys. Furious, he ordered them out without paying her. Then he discovered a prophylactic discarded in the toilet bowl.

Jim called the pastor and told him what happened. The pastor, hearing about the two boys said, "Well, we can rule out love."

Without a doubt, having a baby is quite different today from 50 years ago. Women are much more involved with what happens in the birthing process. In my ninth month, I asked, "What about labor? My gray-haired mustachioed obstetrician replied, "Oh don't worry about that. Leave it to me." Today I would rise up and shout, "Who's about to have this baby? Me. Not you." However, there was nothing to make me ask that question then.

Lamaze labor practices were unknown in my world. For both births, my husband was happy to go home and wait for a call. I was "prepped" in the labor room, examined, and given seconal, which produced amnesia for the next eight hours. As a result, I don't remember much about the labor; and nothing about being in the delivery room, or the actual moment of birth. Christopher, who was expected on December 24, was overdue, so labor was induced on the 29th. While the meds dripped into my arm, the doctor noticed my hands were cold, and remarked, "Why are your hands cold? Don't be afraid. We'll take care of everything."

Sometime later, groggy from the medication, I saw Jim smiling next to me. It took me a minute to realize where I was.

"What was it?"

"A boy," he said, then left to ask the nurse to bring me our nine-pound, nine-ounce baby boy. She held Christopher at the foot of my bed. I stretched out my arms, reaching for him.

"We can't let you hold him. You're too groggy," she said.

The next morning, the after effects of the meds made me and my roommate high. We felt silly while playing with our babies While we were laughing, a man wearing a surgical shirt came in the room and greeted me.

"How are you today Mrs. Russell?"

"Great, who are you?"

"You worked with me quite well yesterday."

"I never saw you before."

"I'm the anesthesiologist."

Considering the size of my baby boy, maybe it was a good thing he had been there, even though I didn't remember it.

My mother had stayed in the maternity hospital for a week before bringing her babies home. I too had a longer stay than women today, who are regularly sent home the next day. Chris was born on the 29th of December, yet it wasn't until on January 2nd that our little family was home together.

Our charming pre-war Tudor apartment in Pelham Manor had wide wooden floors and a huge stone fireplace in a spacious living room, but only one bedroom with our bed and Matt's crib. There was barely space for a bassinet along with a playpen. With two babies in two rooms, I yearned to move into a place with at least two bedrooms.

When Jim found a duplex apartment with a fenced-in yard in White Plains, I was relieved and delighted. The boys had a bedroom all their own, with room for two cribs and later twin beds. I worked sporadically as a substitute teacher to make ends meet. Jim supplemented his speech-teacher income as an assistant coach for football, wrestling and cross country.

Jim was a popular swim pro during summers at the Century Country Club in the Westchester town of Purchase. He taught children from the Lehman, Loeb and Bronfman families how to swim. Edgar Bronfman Jr. once pointed to the Lear jet flying above the pool, saying, "There goes Daddy."

From my perch by the pool, I watched as young mothers flocked around my husband while I rightfully remained in the background with my little boys. Once, I sat in the baby pool next to David Susskind, the pioneer talk show host, who was playing with his young daughter.

After his voice lessons with Luigi in the city, Jim got paid roles in summer theaters in Westchester. He was a fabulous Billy Bigelow in *Carousel*, a charming Harold

Hill in the *Music Man,* and with his full head of black curly hair and sweet baritone, a perfect Curly in *Oklahoma.* His rehearsals went into the early morning hours.

One night, while rehearsing *Pal Joey*, he collapsed, falling off the stage and clutching his heart. They took him to the emergency room and sent him home with instructions to stay in bed and not get up for several days. I was more puzzled than alarmed. What was it? Surely a 36-year-old father and husband couldn't have heart trouble. The doctors said there was no indication of heart disease; it was exhaustion. Soon he was up and back at work, but frightened enough to decide he would never perform on stage again. He never did, except for a couple of solos in community chorus where his stage presence caused the same stir in the audience. We soon forgot about his heart attack scare, glad to have him home a little more often.

Embracing the mystique of the women's movement was hard to do on my back porch during the long summer afternoons. My function was to be there in case one or the other of my two boys broke his leg or got a bloody nose while playing in the neighborhood. My career was on hold, and my master's degree on a shelf while my husband worked and went to classes for his master's. I kept occupied in the summer creating macramé belts while watching the Watergate hearings. There was little opportunity for self-actualization, let alone meaningful employment.

Newcomers in the suburbs were usually greeted by the Welcome Wagon lady. She brought gifts: jar openers with local merchant logos, dishcloths and other domestic items. In addition, she organized monthly gettogethers at each other's houses for crafting sessions. When my neighbor friend and I attended one of those gatherings in our Westchester neighborhood, countering the standards of a patriarchal society was not on my mind.   Seated in a large circle in a comfortable suburban den, we were surrounded by raffia, which we were weaving into small stools when two representatives of the Mount Kisco newspaper appeared brandishing a camera. The photographer took each of our pictures as we finished our projects. Afterwards, the reporter (who obviously didn't relish this assignment) addressed the young woman sitting to my right.

"What's your name?" he queried.

"Susan Brown," she answered.

"Don't you have a husband?" he responded in a voice dripping with scorn.

"Yes, I do." she reassured him.

"Well, what's his name?"

"John."

"Ok, so you are Mrs. John Brown. That's what we need."

Thus, he moved counterclockwise around the room, carefully noting each husband's name, giving me plenty of time to consider what my own response would be.

When he came to me, I boldly replied with my own given name.

"What's your husband's name?" He was quite annoyed.

"He's not here. If you took his picture, would you be asking him my name?" I countered.

"Well, if you don't tell me your husband's name, I can't put your picture in the paper."

Thinking my life was not likely to be hampered by not having my picture in the Society page of the local Mt. Kisco newspaper, I said, "Fine, don't put my picture in the paper."

Gasps came from each corner of the room. I had apparently committed a big faux pas. Without support from the other women in the room, my neighbor and I grabbed our little stools and ran for the door, bursting to let loose our reaction. Safely in the car with the portent of our audacity fresh in our wake, we screamed on the way home like kids running from a Halloween prank.

I'd like to think I made a small contribution to the feminist cause that day with my then - unacceptable behavior. It's been a long time since women's names were identified as their husband's. Even more significant advances are now taken for granted, but sometimes it's good to reflect on how far we've come.

The Think System

In a picture of us taken in the first year of our marriage, I was pregnant and sitting on Jim's lap and smiling sleepily into the camera. We were visiting the home of our best man, Richard and his wife Evelyn, who were older and had no children. Jim was a favorite, so they took me under their wing as well. When Matt was born, they doted on him. Evelyn cooed, "This is the most beautiful baby boy." I had to agree; he was so angelic. We spent some lovely times in their little house in Rye. Sadly, a short five years later, Dick died after a short illness and his widow greeted me brightly after his funeral service. "We had the best marriage. No marriage could be better than ours."

I felt somehow beset by her remark. Would I ever be able to say the same about our marriage? At the time, we were struggling financially on Jim's teacher salary plus coaching jobs while I was keeping up with two toddlers and directing a large nursery school. Each season took Jim away from me and the boys for most of the days and weekends.

After the long summer days as the Swim Pro at the club, when he went back to teach in the fall, he continued coaching cross-country and wrestling in the winter; in addition, he started evening classes at Fordham. I was developing a full-scale depression, but schooled in the advantages of counseling during my graduate work, I saw a psychiatrist who prescribed another prescription that allowed me to continue my juggling act.

I often accused Jim of using the "think system" espoused by Harold Hill, the character he played in *The Music Man*. He had completed all courses for his Master's in Speech at Cornell, but didn't finish because he hadn't written his final research paper. He said he had all the data, so I often nagged him to let me help him finish. I'd gone right from undergraduate to graduate school with an assistantship and earned my Masters before we married, so I expected him to finish his degree since he was so close. When he came home and announced he wanted to be an elementary school principal and was enrolling in graduate school in Fordham University, I was surprised, but delighted with his decision and didn't complain about not being a part of the thinking.

When it was time to buy a house, I was charged with the search, and found a small brick-front ranch in Mount Kisco. When Jim saw it, he chatted with the owners on his own, and told them we'd buy it. Again, he was the decider, but we were now homeowners.

By the time the boys were in nursery school, I had become passionate about early childhood education, becoming a nursery school teacher and soon after, Director. I jumped into the excitement of the new "discovery" approaches that were so much in line with what I was observing about the way my own preschoolers learned. Life as the Director of a large nursery school was quite demanding, especially when dealing with the early morning calls to find substitutes for sick teachers. Along with millions of other young mothers and wives who juggle the demands of the job, I found motherhood and marriage were becoming stressful.

At home in the summers, I taught myself to play guitar; we young mothers had "Hootenannies" in each other's homes with the children playing around us, sometimes singing with us. While Jim worked two and three jobs at a time, our little boys were my greatest joy; they were certainly my companions for most of the days. We devoured many children's books together, creating a neighborhood lending library on the sunroom porch. Our active, growing boys seemed to gang up on me from time to time and Jim was seldom home. I wanted my husband's attention more than it was possible for him to extend it. Such expectations led to disappointment because when Jim was home, he was either studying or sleeping.

However, he loved having people to the house for parties and I willingly obliged. I would prepare the food, and he'd set up the drinks. After the party, he cleaned up, but I went to bed because I couldn't drink much before becoming sleepy and useless.

The "think system" was in place again years later when he informed me and all our friends he was having a vasectomy. The band teacher in the high school was from the south. He talked about getting his vasectomy and then played the French horn with the New Haven Symphony the next night. He complained, "You don't know what "stingin" is until you've played the horn for the Brahms #4 after a vasectomy."

Two birth control methods we used had failed, resulting in two pregnancies, but now the pill was working fine, so I was surprised to learn about his appointment. Jim entertained his friends by describing how one of his doctor buddies stopped by to chat about sports while he was getting "clipped."

Although the vasectomy had been entirely his decision, it was my tacit understanding he wanted to prevent any more surprise pregnancies. Born in August under the sign of Leo, astrologists would say he was the benevolent ruler who needed to avoid additional fatherhood responsibilities. He and he was still contributing to Ed's support in California, so his decision trumped any desire I might have had for another baby. In the end, he was right; our family was complete and I was content to be the mother of two fine sons and a Principal's wife for the next seventeen years.

Our small house in Westchester sold quickly when we moved to in the Adirondacks. Having finished his Master's; newly certified, he became the Saranac Lake elementary school principal for their four schools scattered throughout the North Country. We found our three-bedroom mortgaged white shingled house on the side of Dewey mountain. Our boys would walk over the mountain to school, ride their bikes to town and make lifelong friends. Jim and I planted welcoming bushes and flowers on the rock wall along our driveway. We loved to hold end of the school year parties for his teaching staff.

One year, we were entertained by a beautiful belly dancer. The nearby lakes beckoned and I learned to sail. Jim bought me a used Sunfish sailboat which we stored on a friend's dock on Lake Kiwassa where I spent lovely hours chasing the wind and participating in local races each Sunday in the summer.

Most of my dissatisfaction as the Principal's wife was that I couldn't get hired by the school system for a full-time position. While working part-time, I followed my passion for early childhood by taking courses in teaching reading to gain certification in the early grades. When I applied for a temporary position teaching kindergarten in one of Jim's schools, I remember vividly what the superintendent told me, "The Board of Education doesn't want me to hire any more spouses; we already have too many husbands and wives on the payroll."

The issue was settled. Refusing employment based on a marriage relationship was clearly against today's personnel practices, but at the time, I could do nothing. Hiring a lawyer and bringing a grievance would be difficult today, but then, making any fuss while my husband was a Principal in the system was not an option. I finally obtained a full-time position not funded by Jim's school system, providing speech/language therapy in several different school systems throughout the

Adirondacks. Because I drove many miles to several different schools served by the Board of Education each week, it was hard to feel I really belonged anywhere. It was also difficult to establish a strong relationship with individual children or the staff.

Yet, outside of my part-time work in the schools, our marriage fostered huge helpings of opportunity for me. Jim enjoyed being at home with the boys in the evenings; he was determined to keep his vow to avoid performing in productions that might land him in the hospital as it had when he was performing in summer theatre in Westchester. His need to be home in the evenings enabled me to join community theatre and choral groups that one wouldn't ordinarily expect to find in a village surrounded by high peaks and winter sports.

One season, in Saranac Lake, I had a role in the North Country Community College's production *of Godspell,* the great rock opera, where I sang and danced with the group. Each season in nearby Lake Placid, we mounted wonderful musical theatre productions. *In The Music Man*, I realized my long-held ambition to play Marion, the Librarian. In *A Funny Thing Happened on the Way to the Forum*, I was Philia, Pseudolus' harridan wife. For that role, I loved finding ways to make the audience laugh, a buoyant new experience for me as a performer.

Through the Lake Placid connection, I was asked to audition for the strangest role of my life. I starred as the unicorn in a 1978 production of *Santa Claus and the Unicorn,* written by Julie Adams Strandberg for the

Dance Theatre of Harlem. The role had previously been played by a dancer who they said had been too sexy to be cavorting with Santa, and her voice wasn't that good. With me, they got a singer who had no idea how to be a sexy unicorn, but I did my best at being an awkward, sad one. After we played the Lake Placid Center for Music and Art, we joined the Harlem dance company's production at City College of New York, just a block from Broadway, albeit 96 blocks uptown from 42nd Street. The harpist from Lake Placid was the accompanist for all the music.

Santa Claus was played by a white man in Lake Placid, but a black man sang the role in Harlem. The audience didn't know what color I was, since my head was ensconced in a *papier mache* unicorn head with a megaphone mouth and I was dressed in a white leotard, with a furry white tail behind. *Tour pour l'art.*

For seventeen summers, the Adirondacks were filled with learning new music in daily voice lessons and sight-singing classes. We also performed great choral works by Durefle, Mozart, Faure, Vivaldi, Brubeck, along with Gregg Smith's *Magnificat* with the Gregg Smith Singers. Jim was always in the audience and helped entertain the singers and guest artists at our receptions after each concert. Along the way, we established friendships to cherish the rest of our lives.

The First and Last Miss Rensselaer

Jim always liked to reveal my past as a Miss America Pageant contestant, but I would never mention it. Over the years since I became a widow, I've seldom revealed my history as Miss New York State to new friends and acquaintances. It seems the whole experience happened to someone else, except for the second week each September when "There she is, Miss America" is sung again in Atlantic City.

Despite recent attempts at revival in Las Vegas, The Miss America Pageant has moved back to Atlantic City; a new Miss America will be crowned in the place where it began. When I was a girl it was the most popular television broadcast each second Saturday in September. Late that night, television screens all over the country tuned in to watch contestants from each state compete. We girls all dreamed of becoming Miss America.

The Pageant has always been controversial. When it started in 1921, Atlantic City businessmen were trying to keep tourists in town after Labor Day; it was strictly a leg-show then. Billed as the "Bather's Revue," it was a two-day event that culminated in a beachfront parade. But to keep it "decent," a board of censors was installed to make sure the bathing suits of the day were of the proper length. As the years passed, more rules were applied. Not only did the girls have to be at least 18 years old, only white girls could enter. Some criticisms appeared with the advent of feminism and civil rights, so the Pageant was reformed, black girls entered and a few, like Vanessa Williams, have walked down the runway as Miss America.

These contestants were not there because they were especially pretty. They needed to be talented, graceful and worthy of a scholarship to "further their education." In short, they were the epitome of the words Bert Parks sang as the new Miss America made her way down the long ramp into the cheering audience:

> *There she is, Miss America*
> *There she is, your ideal*
> *The dream of a million girls who are more than pretty can come true in Atlantic City*
> *For she may turn out to be the Queen of Femininity*
> *There she is your ideal...*

As sophomore at Albany State Teachers college, now SUNY Albany, I was commuting to classes from Rensselaer across the Hudson River from Albany. I'd shown some aptitude for teaching, although singing was still my first love and I needed those voice lessons. Finding the extra money each week as a student was an extra expense. Consequently, I entered the Miss Albany contest because it provided a small "scholarship that I could use for my lessons. It is hard to recall much about that first competition in 1957, except that I was the runner-up. Afterwards, I told myself, "Nice try, but now back to real life."

The following year, the Rensselaer Junior Chamber of Commerce Chairman, Don Leahey, called to tell me "We're having the first Miss Rensselaer contest, and you should enter! You entered in Albany; surely you should be in your hometown contest."

I thought, "I'm through with that pageant stuff, and I'm busy with college." But somehow, the allure of the Miss America pageant and my girlish dreams won out. With my friend's' urging, I entered the first and last Miss Rensselaer Pageant as a veteran contestant and won it. I was on my way to the Miss New York State Pageant the next weekend.

There are three parts to a Miss America Pageant: a "personality" competition, where the judges have a friendly conversation with each girl; a "poise" competition, requiring a straight back and a glide around the stage in an evening gown; a talent competition and the dreaded "swimsuit" competition.

One can overcome trepidations about the "swimsuit" portion of the program by concentrating on the "pivot." This maneuver was done by walking carefully in three-inch heels to center stage, stopping to smile, putting one foot forward, then by raising both heels slightly, make a 180 degree turn. Repeat once more, smiling at the judges while wishing you were somewhere else.

Converted to a community college now, in 1958 the Van Curler Hotel was Schenectady's finest building. Our families and friends gathered in the auditorium with Chamber of Commerce sponsors from across the state.

One contestant from Nassau county, looked just like blonde, sultry Kim Novak, of Hitchcock movie fame. Her talent was dress designing. She appeared in a tight, fire-engine red knit dress topped with a matching beret. She could easily have been the winner, but as she stepped in front of the microphone to answer the single question put to her, she repeated the question and then a curtain of silence descended upon her. Nothing came out of her mouth.

At my turn, I gave a glib answer about combating "juvenile delinquency" with education. If "Kim Novak" had spoken, she would be on her way to Atlantic City instead of me. As a result, I'm certain I won by default.

It was a thrill to be robed and crowned, then swathed in a diagonal banner; being "Miss New York, 1958" felt wonderful. I vowed to give it my all.

The next week, I returned to classes at college where a photographer from the local paper took pictures of my day in classes and socializing between, I was summoned to the dean's office. A straight-laced Quaker, he asked, "Do you really want this leg show on your resume?"

This put me on the defensive, and I rose to all of my five feet two inches and declared, "I just won a scholarship sponsored by Pepsi-Cola that will pay for an on-campus residency next year in the Beta Zeta sorority house, while I do my practice teaching in the campus school. Furthermore, I am honored to be representing the great Empire State at the Miss America Pageant."

His question was prescient, though. I have never used my dubious honor as Miss New York on any of my resumes since graduate school. When I was awarded my assistantship at the University of Connecticut for graduate studies, one of my professors remarked that he hadn't heard of a Pepsi-Cola Scholarship before.

Assuredly, they've probably not heard of it since.

That summer was a blur of preparation; I exercised faithfully and practiced singing. Looking for a song to impress the Pageant judges I chose Gershwin's "Summertime," a simple song that seemed fit my voice at the time.

Appearances were scheduled, and gowns ordered.

"Sunny," a local TV personality, co-hosted the New York State Pageant. She was chosen to be my Atlantic City chaperone and came equipped with a news camera.

Mother-chaperones were not allowed, so my family drove separately to New Jersey while I traveled with Sunny and Don Leahey, the Rensselaer Junior Chamber of Commerce President.

On the way to Atlantic City, we stopped in New York, where a small group of contestants appeared on the nationally televised *Ed Sullivan Show*. Each of us walked toward the camera, smiled, and said our name and state. Everyone in the audience was impressed with Mary Ann Mobley, Miss Mississippi's charming Southern drawl. Notably, in Mississippi, they really knew how to grow Miss America contestants: Mississippi girls were nurtured and rehearsed into a polished act with thousands of dollars invested in coaches and pageant training. Miss Mississippi won two consecutive Miss America crowns as a result.

Sunny installed me in the hotel and spent time with the other news people; consequently, I seldom saw her. I spent the week preparing for nightly competitions in the four preliminary categories. There was one particularly strict rule about behavior: I was not allowed to have any association with men, including my father.

Prior to the competition, The Albany Knickerbocker News asked me to write about my experiences in Atlantic City. Each night I wrote about the day, reading the dispatch for publication to an editor from my hotel phone.

I wrote about the "personality" competition when Contestants ate breakfast in small groups, while judges moved from table to table. A starry pantheon of judges included Moss Hart, Kitty Carlisle, Bennett Cerf, and Mitch Miller. While he and Kitty Carlisle were at my table, I told Moss Hart that I was thrilled to meet him since I had seen a production of his play, *The Man Who Came to Dinner* when I was just eleven. He seemed offended that I'd pointed out how long ago his play had been written and produced, countering, "Really, I've weathered rather well."

Trying to impress Mitch Miller, of TV singalongs with the bouncing ball fame, I said that playing the saxophone in the high school band helped me with breath control for singing. He was unimpressed; so I bombed the breakfast interview with him.

One article I wrote was about the boardwalk parade at the start of the pageant. Before climbing on the back of individual white convertibles, we all gathered in a warehouse-sized dressing room replete with a little table and mirror for each of us. Time magazine took a picture of some of us around those tables, but only my elbow appeared in the corner of the photo. Anita Bryant, Miss Oklahoma, was constantly singing choruses of "Oooohklahoma," and we all joined in.

I noticed a big jar of Vaseline on her dressing table. "Just smear it on your upper gums, and your face won't get tired," she explained. It worked — you can smile for miles because your upper lip slides up your teeth. Newly slathered and beaming, we all grinned constantly for several hours while waving elegantly at the crowds lining the boardwalk.

At the enormous convention center, we met our host, the inimitable Bert Parks, known as the guy with "the smile you can read by." Present for each of the preliminary competitions, Bert beamed and chatted with us as we took turns rehearsing.

After rehearsing "Summertime" once with the orchestra, I wanted to repeat it, needing to get used to that huge space, but we were all allowed only one run through, which made me feel quite unsure of myself. At that night's judging, I had two measures of introduction to move from the curtain to the stage apron microphone.

It still seems like I'd never made it, but my scrapbook photo shows me in front of the mike. I must have come close enough.

On the televised final Pageant night, my panic mounted. Overcome with nerves, it was the only time in my life I was too anxious to eat. I was exhausted and thinner than ever. When the announcement of the final ten contestants who'd compete in the live broadcast that Saturday was made, it didn't include me. My disappointment was tempered with relief as I settled back to my spectator position in the back of the stage with the other contestants who hadn't made the top ten.

Miss Mississippi, Mary Ann Mobley wowed the judges with a few measures from Puccini, and then whipped off her skirt for a sexy dance to "There's Gonna be Some Changes Made." She was polished and professional. All I knew how to do was stand up and sing without a microphone. Later, her soft-drawled responses to judges' questions won her vital points over Anita Bryant, the runner-up.

Returning home to "finish my reign in New York State" became a series of "crown and gown" appearances. In addition to the crown and gown, I wore long sleeve gloves for store openings and visits to children's hospitals. I have a press photo of me with Governor Harriman, shaking his hand wearing a pair of those long white gloves plus crown. Sometimes those gloves came in handy, especially when handing out roses at a supermarket opening. Looking at all those photos now, though, it seems odd to be wearing a crown on my head so ubiquitously.

As Miss New York, I became the first person in my family to fly anywhere on a plane. For the opening of a Pepsi bottling plant, both Mother and Dad watched me climb the stairs onto the plane. I waved at them through the small window where I pressed my nose feeling the lightness of the take-off for the first time. I will never forget that first uplift and that flight over the Adirondacks in autumn with trees ablaze in color. Pepsi provided dress material printed with their red, white and blue logo—my mother sewed it quickly for that excursion. Despite wearing that strange dress, I was thrilled.

As for dresses, there may be nothing wrong with wearing a hoop-skirted, ruffled strapless Miss America ball gown to throw out a hockey puck in middle of an ice hockey stadium. However, when my photo appeared in *Sports Illustrated* magazine, my outfit was called "froufrou finery." Maybe it *was* a silly outfit to wear for the occasion.

Of all those activities, I am most proud of my local television interview with my favorite instructor, Dr. Paul Pettit, a professor in the Theatre Department at Albany. I asked him to talk about a new theatre in the round at the college. Along with the other college faculty, he seemed astounded that I could interview him appropriately on the air. In those days, expectations for girls were not very high; it seemed that when a "beauty queen" did an adequate job, it was surprising.

Another professor who read my daily newspaper articles asked if I was the one who had really written the stories appearing on the front page with my picture. She was unimpressed with my previous performance in her short story class, so she asked me if I had written them; I assured her the articles were completely accurate accounts and indeed I had written them all myself.

In the back of my mind, I was learning that a Miss America contestant was not a universally recognized grand achievement. Nonetheless, I hadn't expected to be summarily pre-judged as an air-head.

At one of our "crown and gown" appearances, Lee Ann Meriwether came into the changing room, rushing to dress. "I heard there's going to be steak for dinner—I can't wait. I'm starving." Lee Ann was Miss America in 1955, before joining the Today show and TV roles on *Barnaby Jones*, and *All My Children*. However, while launching her acting career, she was on the verge of starving. After meeting Lee Ann, I dumped the idea of show business as a career, and filled out applications for graduate school assistantships.

Joan Crawford looked like she was starving when we were introduced at a Pepsi Cola convention. She was a tiny thing, bird-like, wearing a matching silver and black print dress and pillbox hat. This was before the *Mommy Dearest* book and movie and I was quite stars-truck by her, especially when she said, "That color looks beautiful on you," while admiring my magenta velvet cocktail dress. I burbled a quiet "Thank you" while trying to digest a compliment from a real movie star.

Watching the pageant in ensuing years, embarrassment crept in. I was offended when a young woman answered a question about women's roles, saying "I do feel that a woman's place is in the home with her husband and with her children." Even without the new awareness of the feminist movement, I had come from a long line of working women who managed to balance the necessity of careers with motherhood. I no longer wanted to be associated with that kind of young woman whose view of life was so limited.

As a past Miss New York, friends would call me the day after the Pageant to ask if I thought Miss Kansas should have won over Miss California, but I hadn't bothered to turn it on. Eventually I stopped watching the Miss America pageant altogether, along with millions of other Americans. It still attracted talented, beautiful accomplished women, but with an ambiguity that also represents what some might call an "old-fashioned" view. Others view it as misogynistic.

The Miss America Pageant no longer spoke to what I was becoming or cared about. I was *Another Mother for Peace* during Vietnam and wore the necklace engraved with, "War is not healthy for children and other living things." Later becoming the Principal's wife and a teacher were new identities that changed my values and defined my life. Indeed, I could no longer justify this "beauty queen" venture. The Rensselaer Junior Chamber of Commerce must have felt the same, since they have never sponsored another pageant to choose another Miss Rensselaer.

Rockin' Through the Rockies

For our 20th wedding anniversary, Jim and I headed for California by way of a rail trip through the Canadian Rockies. When our flight from Montreal landed at the edge of the prairie in Calgary, we went directly to the Canadian Pacific Railway station for the short trip to Banff, where we spent the night. In the morning, we walked the wide flat main street leading to the abrupt vertical rising of a line of cliffs towering over us, our first glimpse of the Rockies. They seemed to be pushing the town into the prairie like the front of a snowplow.

That August afternoon we boarded the train again, continuing west to storied Lake Louise and its grand old hotel, built in the 1920s to attract railway passengers. All the guest-room windows framed a calendar view of a glacier and the ice blue lake beneath it.

The next day we headed west over the Rockies to Vancouver. Scurrying to the observation car, we viewed the tunnels and curves ahead with awe, wondering how the train made it through the narrow passages in winter snows. As the summer day closed into evening darkness, we realized the main purpose of our trip to see the Rockies would soon end. After an evening meal in the dining car, we found our Pullman sleeper, with bunks behind heavy brown curtains on both sides of the aisle. Jim and I started out together in the bottom bunk. The moon peeked through the wide window, between breaks in the mountains. I began to realize there wasn't enough room in that bunk for both of us when Jim fell asleep.

I climbed the ladder and crawled into the top bunk. The curve of the ceiling, inches from my face, was like the inside of a metal coffin. Trying to ignore the concept, I turned on my side as the jiggling motion of the car continued unabated, shaking my body as if someone were trying to wake me. There would be no sleep for me that night on the train still rocking through the Rockies. At dawn, Jim was still sleeping when I heard the porter pass by. I was quite thirsty and tried to get down, but the ladder was gone. Sticking my hand between the curtains, I whimpered, "Could I please have a drink of water?" The porter kindly brought me a small glass. When the train finally pulled into Vancouver, it was a relief to be stationary.

Soon we were off to Victoria for a brief tour of the gardens, where we especially admired the gigantic roses. Knowing I was exhausted and sleep-deprived, Jim suggested we take the ocean ferry to Seattle that night rather than stay in Canada. Another evening was falling around us as we crossed over in the sunset. Disembarking, a customs agent asked for our birthplace. Joining the line of others headed back to the states, I proudly stated: "Albany, New York."

All I wanted was a quiet room with a bed. The Seattle Hilton did not disappoint. No guest, before or since, could appreciate its thick carpets and enormous cushiony bed with three gigantic pillows as much as I did that night. To top it off, in the morning, we indulged in room service where I had my first bowl of granola with yogurt and fresh fruit. It was a discovery I've enjoyed many times for breakfast since and it always reminds me of our rockin' anniversary trip that year.

No Day at the Beach

One Easter vacation we went to Acapulco to meet Chris. He was spending a semester in Mexico where his fluent Spanish would help us through any language barrier. I had always wanted to go to Acapulco, where Jackie and JFK honeymooned high above the harbor. Our hotel wasn't on the hillside with a view of the city and huge bay where cruise ships docked, but down on the Acapulco Bay beach.

Our balcony overlooked the pool and the beach. For most of the day, a Mariachi band played, their boisterous Latin sound echoing off the hotel walls. The first few days seemed like being in the movie "10," but after a while, we longed for something more secluded and cleaner. Trash floated onto the beach from the sea, and militia men in uniform patrolled the beaches with rifles slung on their backs, adding a menacing touch to the scene. Out on the street in front of the hotel, indigenous women sat on the sidewalks holding out their hands for money as their infants slept on their laps.

From our balcony, I could see a broad sandy beach on the far spit of lush land at the tip of the bay. It looked clean and inviting – a distant, possibly accessible Shangri-La.

"Let's go there. It looks deserted. We can rent one of those tourist Jeeps."

Chris and Jim agreed and we three set off, leaving the congestion and beggars of old Acapulco behind and drove into the jungle on a narrow dirt road—apparently, the only route to the end of the peninsula.

The hot sun beat down on our skin in the open Jeep while we wished we'd brought something to drink. I was impatient to jump in the water to cool off, but so far there were no other roads or signs leading to the beach, but we continued, slowly jolting over the deep ruts.

"There. Over there on the side of the road, it's smooth, no ruts." I pointed out a strip of level dirt on the right. As soon as we pulled onto the smooth area, we were hubcap-deep, mired in dry, soft sand, wheels spinning – stuck on a secluded jungle road. Where was that beach?

Jim jumped out on one side of the jeep and Chris on the other. I stayed seated, scowling behind my sunglasses thinking, "It's a trap. We're stuck here, snared like rabbits, and it looks like there is no way to get out."

Jim looked past me to Chris on the other side of the jeep and asked, "Where did you get that shovel?"

"From this kid," he answered as a boy appeared with a couple of wide boards.

"Thank goodness," Jim said.

"Please may we use those boards? Here, I have pesos; I'll pay."

A grown man appeared with another shovel.

"Who's he?" Jim asked Chris, who was speaking to the two in Spanish.

"I think it's this kid's father. He'll help us dig."
"Great. Tell him we'll pay." Jim was pulling bills out of his pocket to illustrate how he would reward them.

"Wait a minute, guys," I thought, "these people have us trapped here. It was deliberate, and now you're going to pay them?" I was becoming annoyed at Jim's naiveté.

"I'm sure it wasn't deliberate," he said.

"Anyway, we're stuck."

Chris, along with the father and son on his side of the car, started to dig, creating room for the wheels to sink deeper into the loose sand. A truck suddenly appeared with a dozen men standing up in the back. It pulled in front of us.

"Ask them if they have a chain. Tell them I'll pay," Jim offered, pulling more bills from his pockets. The men in the truck produced a chain, attached it to the front of the Jeep, and pulled us out onto solid ground in a jiffy. All open palms were soon covered with paper bills; the chain was removed and the truck disappeared as suddenly as it had appeared.

I hadn't forgotten about our mission—the beach and a swim in the surf. The father and son pointed through the jungle, telling Chris there was a place to change and beyond, at last — a short walk to the beach. Meanwhile, they would supply us with a warm Pepsi and wash the Jeep with a trickling hose lying on the ground. Jim took all offers while Chris and I went on ahead.

We found the beach deserted, but clean and inviting, and beyond, the roiling surf. We looked back toward Acapulco in the distance. I rushed down the steep dune, put one foot into the water, and was immediately pulled down by a strong undertow. Losing control of my body, I instantly somersaulted under for a frightening moment before coming up for air. Still unable to find my footing, I yelled and stretched out my hand. "Help!" Chris stood only inches away from the maelstrom on the sharp incline of the dune when he grabbed my hand. His grip held tight as he pulled me out of the churning waves gasping for breath.

We clambered up to Jim, who was standing at the top of the dune, oblivious of my near-drowning.

"Chris saved my life. I went under right there.

The riptide knocked me completely over and I couldn't stand. He had to pull me out, before my head was mashed to mush on the bottom." I blubbered.

Jim smiled under his sunglasses and turned to leave. "OK, ready?"

"Now I know why this place is deserted. It's too dangerous."

I wanted Jim to acknowledge the close call, to say something like, "Sorry this happened. I know you are disappointed you can't swim in the water, but at least you didn't drown." We were extracted from the roadside trap; the Jeep was cleaned up and all was ready for the return to the hubbub of Acapulco. He had protected us all he could.

Italy At Last

Jim, the Italophile, was able to indulge his passion with only one trip to Italy. With our friends John and Novi Goldsmith, we signed up for the usual grand tour starting in Rome. As soon as we found our room in the hotel, he was off exploring the neighborhood. I settled in our room to call Jean Pedro Mattino. My friend Phyllis and her husband hosted him and the Italian ski team during the 1980 Lake Placid Olympics. They had kept in touch and remained friends. When Phyllis, a world-class knitter, heard we were going to Rome, she gave me his phone number and asked if I would call and give him the baby sweater she had just finished for his grandchild.

Jean Pedro answered the phone. I explained who I was and my mission to deliver the gift. "Where are you?" he asked? "I'll be right over." I quickly repaired my makeup and rushed to the small lobby to greet him. Jean Pedro arrived looking like he stepped out of a New York

Times Magazine ad for Gucci suits. He was slim as a male model, with impeccable continental manners and spoke English with a wonderful Italian accent. Momentarily, Jim arrived in his Bermuda shorts and white sport socks topped with red stripes. Tennis shoes and boat hat completed the clown-like outfit. He too was bowled over by Jean Pedro's splendid persona. Later Jim described him as so dashing he could have "kissed him on the lips." Somehow, Jim could say these rather scandalous things and people would laugh.

"My family is at our beach place this week while I'm still here at work in Rome. Let me take you to dinner tonight," he offered.

"We are traveling with another couple," I explained.

"Bring them along. I'll be back in an hour." After he left, we were stunned for a moment before we called John and Novi to tell about our dashing new Italian guide. Then we hurried to our suitcases to pull out the best clothes we had with us.

Precisely one hour later, Franco came and whisked us away in his shiny black BMW. Soon we were seated at a table outdoors in a travel-poster piazza. The fountain in the center burbled away as we got to know our host, who helped us order an epicurean antipasto and then the most extraordinary tender pasta with tomato sauce.

After we learned that Jean Pedro was still a passionate ski team sponsor on Italy's Olympic Committee, John asked him point blank, "What do you do?"

"I'm with the World Bank."

Our jaws dropped and eyes widened. We were at a loss to say anything pertaining to that institution; it was far out of the sphere of our parochial lives, although we were aware of its global significance in providing financial and technical aid to impoverished countries.

Jean Pedro rescued the conversation. "Let me show you the Forum." It is beautiful at night. The ancient illuminated columns were still intact, closer to immortality than humanity. Leaving the glow of the lighted columns, we walked back to the parking area, where Jean Pedro pressed a button on his key ring and treated use to the first winking headlights we had seen. Now they are common, but in 1991, it was unusual enough for him to remark, "It's happy to see me." Indeed, we were also. He gave us the most wonderful introduction to Italy.

After visiting the storied tourist sites in Rome, Florence and environs, we continued to Venice where we marveled at the waterways, tiny shops filled with Venetian glass and casual outdoor eateries in St. Mark's Square. The façade of St. Mark's and the regularity of the arches of the Doge's Palace were romantic and lovely. Nevertheless, I was surprised by my reaction when I entered St. Marks. The church was under reconstruction at the time with scaffolding throughout; it was dark and reeking of incense, making me a bit nauseated. I fled back into the sunshine and waited for Jim and the others before visiting the enormous Doge's Palace next door.

The great wide stairway led into the Sala del Maggior Consiglio (the Hall of the Great Council), which was dominated by a frieze featuring the first doges of Venice. Each one held a scroll documenting his personal achievements. Almost two stories high, the Doge portraits were presented against a black background. Up in a high corner was a tiny crucifix, glowing against the dark. The Doges appeared to set themselves larger than Christ—a frightful distinction. It spoke of the arrogant wielding of power. The Council is reputed to be a bastion of Republicanism in the sense that any male adult in the aristocracy was allowed to serve, but I was offended. Leaving the others to admire the 16th century glorification of power, I crossed over the famed Bridge of Sighs to the adjacent prison.

Truly, the condemned must have sighed heavily as they were led from the spacious palace to the dark cells. I found myself alone in a small cell with bars. Moving out of the first one, I was in another cell and then another until I thought I couldn't find my way out. My usual independent courage left me and I called out until Jim and the others found me and we made our way back into the sunshine of the square again. It didn't seem to matter to my companions that while visiting the epicenter of Western culture, I was sickened by the first building, intimidated by the next and frightened by the third.

Jim's Dream

I shared my enthusiasm for bird identification with Jim after I took an ornithology course, and we started visiting wildlife refuges. He soon became more enthusiastic about bird-watching than I had been. We visited the Assateague National Wildlife Refuge at Chincoteague Island, Virginia, where the pretty ducks and magnificent snow geese gathered in great gaggles. Jim was determined to move near there when he retired, but I had my reservations.

Over 25 years of married life, Jim's dream was to retire as early as possible. He had an increasing thirst to get out from the stress of being the principal of four elementary schools and live in a less harsh climate than the Adirondacks. I really didn't want to leave the place where our sons had grown up. I had put down firm roots, but his need was stronger. Inadvertently, by bringing him to the refuge, I provided the impetus that fleshed out his dream to move to the Eastern Shore of Virginia.

With his retirement close at hand, we visited Chincoteague and the Wildlife Refuge at Assateague Island to look around. To me, the houses on the mainland in Chincoteague seemed too crowded together in contrast to the privacy of our mountainside home in the North Country. It was hard for me to match Jim's enthusiasm for the idea of moving there, but I told friends, "I don't want to rain on his parade."

"You are his parade." one answered. That stopped my complaints and I agreed to buy a funny, lopsided house that he loved in a harbor town on the Eastern Shore of the Chesapeake Bay. Jim's dream was to renovate it as they did on the TV show, *This Old House.*

As soon as we moved in that fall, he hired local workmen and enjoyed toiling alongside them to improve the old place. In the afternoons while I was working at a nearby school, he'd walk down to the harbor with his binoculars and watch the ospreys tending their nests high up on the bay markers.

He loved the garage workshop where he refinished furniture and built ship models while listening to his opera recordings. I was happy working as an itinerant speech therapist in the county schools, and in the summer, I enjoyed membership in the Eastern Shore Country Club where I played tennis and led water aerobics.

Things were going well until I jumped up to return a ball on the tennis court and came down on my heel, snapping my Achilles tendon. Jim arrived shortly after the ambulance and followed it to the hospital. I was given a choice of a cast or surgery. When I learned that there was a 12-week recovery for each remedy, I opted for the cast. Three months later, finally out of the cast, I was tentatively exercising my tender tendon in the pool. Coming out, I stepped on a poolside pebble and snapped it again. I knew the sound—like a balloon popping. Fortunately, our good friends Bob and Jean Martin happened to arrive just as I slid to the poolside. When Jim arrived, they formed a hand-chair and lifted me to our car instead of calling the ambulance. On our way toward the hospital, Jim said, "I've got to make a stop at the house. I left the insurance card there,"

"Hey," I said, "next time when they call you from the club and they tell you 'Miriam is down,' bring the card with you."

He quipped, "The next time they call me from the club and tell me 'Miriam is down,' I'm going to say, 'Miriam who?'"

At last, they performed a surgical repair on my Achilles. It was another 12 weeks before I could walk around the block by myself with a cane.

I recently developed plantar fasciitis in both feet unable to walk or stand for more than a short time. Dealing with a debilitating predicament on my own without him, I realized how much Jim did for me during my long year of recovery from the Achilles surgery. Was I appreciative at the time? Did I show enough gratitude for the meals, the cleaning, and the shopping he did that made my life comfortable? Over the years, recalling his solicitousness, I regret I didn't tell him more often that I knew how well he cherished me.

We did argue. I could never convince him of my side, feeling he always thought he'd done nothing wrong to apologize for. I accused him of never saying "I'm sorry." during one of our squabbles about a matter so small I can't remember the details. Our usual custom was not to "make up" after an argument because we just waited for it to blow over. But once after a disagreement, when I was hobbling around at school on crutches, he sent me a huge bouquet of roses with a card signed, "I'm sorry." I loved him more then. His thoughtfulness eased any concerns about our marriage. On one hand, I expected more closeness, on the other, I appreciated the space and freedom we gave each other.

Jim often complained I was too "complicated." It's true that love ebbs and flows in a marriage. It's sad to think how little we notice when it swells for a moment; then we feel helpless with admiration and appreciation, not sharing the feeling. It's too easy to let the moment pass, without grabbing it and folding it into the relationship, forgetting the echoes of Arthur Miller's *Death of a Salesman:* "Attention must be paid." Death makes the admonition so important; there might be no more chances to pay that attention.

Starting Over

After almost 30 years, just when we were beginning to develop more closeness as a married couple, Jim's life ended and my single life began. In a way, I was prepared for it because my husband had encouraged everything I did: choral music, voice lessons, community theater, additional college courses, water aerobics, sailing, and work. In addition, he insisted I obtain my own bank accounts, loans and credit cards. He was my biggest cheerleader.

Shortly after we moved to Virginia, I had found a brochure for a doctoral program from Nova Southeastern University in Florida. It was a blended model, partly accessible through the newly available internet. The educational leadership curriculum sounded appealing and the distance learning piece was perfect for someone working full time. Classes met once a month as a cluster in Virginia while weeklong summer seminars in Florida were held when my schools were on vacation.

Even so, at the time it was not for me to get a doctorate, I told Jim. "It is rather costly, especially since you're retired and I'm still working. If we spend time and money, it should be something we can do together." He agreed.

Talking with mother after the funeral, I remembered that program. She listened as I became more excited at the prospect.

"You see, Mom, there is nothing stopping me from doing this now. I need something to keep my mind focused–something hard."

I learned this a common response among the bereaved who feel like flotsam and jetsam in a strange stream. I needed a project I could sink myself in, so I applied for the doctoral program, was accepted and waited for the program to put together enough applicants to create a cluster cohort in Alexandria Virginia.

In 1995, I began the Educational Leadership Doctoral program at Nova Southeastern University, commencing three years that marked my introduction to a new life and career. This program would be hard, but tangible, with specific goals and projects for each term. I would make one very close friend, Donna Martin Hinkle, who often housed me after day-long seminars in Arlington, Virginia. Most of all, it would be a way forward, somewhere I could keep growing and learning in my new chapter as a single woman.

Chapter III

Bumper Car Rides

What people are ashamed about
Usually makes a good story.

F. Scott Fitzgerald

Angry and Obnoxious

Friends, family and acquaintances dutifully invited me to their dinner parties where I found myself irritated and irritating to be the single "fifth wheel." Once I forgot I had accepted an invitation, but they called when I didn't show up.

"Oh, sorry, sorry."

I dressed quickly and drove several miles to the party, finding it filled with married couples. Most of the men were long-time retirees from the Navy.

Later, the conversation turned to politics.

"Welfare is ruining the country," one veteran sailor remarked.

After a drink, I felt like arguing.

"The largest welfare in history was the GI bill. It created the middle class."

I felt more and more as if under siege, especially from the men. Granted, I was hardly a charming dinner companion, but I was also convinced my single status somehow threatened them. Perhaps it was an unconscious fear that they might make widows of their own wives.

Last to arrive, I was the first to leave. Driving home by myself on dark country roads, I hated my new aloneness. I remembered how Jim usually drove while sometimes I fell asleep with my head in his lap.

I was also feeling estranged from many of the women faculty at work. When the feminist issue of equality in the workplace was being discussed in the lunchroom, one Southern-born gal drawled, "I'd just rather be *cherished.*"

Rage rose in my throat again, "You are just one heartbeat away from not being cherished." I said. "You may be safe and comfortable now, protected from the world by your husband, but someday, it's quite likely he'll be gone."

She assumed, as I had, life would continue in the manner to which she had been accustomed. In all likelihood, it wouldn't, therefore before the grim reaper's appearance, women should be given fair opportunities to achieve on their own. Having some portion of good sense left, I kept these thoughts to myself.

I read Joan Didion's memoir, *The Year of Magical Thinking*, about her husband's sudden death. When it was transformed into a one-woman Broadway play, I was in the audience when Vanessa Redgrave addressed us as a Cassandra, "This happened on December 30, 2003. That may seem a while ago, but when it happens to you. *And it will happen to you....*" I wondered what I would have thought, if I had heard those words prior to Jim's death. From the distance of ten years as a widow, there was bitter truth in her speech.

I had given up my foolish youthful certainty that bad things weren't going to happen to me. Death changed my emotional landscape. The comfort and certitude of my marriage was gone; "it" had happened to me, but since it had, and I was still alive and used to being a part of a man's life, could there still be *someone out there for me?* The inevitable question from well-intentioned friends was, "Are you seeing anyone?" Next, I heard, "You'll find someone." It was a vision I found agreeable at the time, but deep inside, I knew it was probably a fallacy that "someone" would make my life happier, wealthier and more fulfilling. Nevertheless, as an outsider in an alien world of couples, looking for a relationship seemed a reasonable venture. I should have resisted the idea in spite of my friends' urgings, but I was becoming a sucker for the *Cinderella Complex.* That book by Colette Dowling, published in 1981, explored the idea that deepdown, women feared independence. Slipping easily into the looking-for-Prince-Charming mode, I truly felt that fear.

For me, in those days, being alive meant the possibility of meeting someone new, someone who would fill the hole in my life left by the loss of a partner for almost 30 years, someone who could make me forget that I was a widow. It would be a new era. Life as I knew it had crumbled, but it had to be rebuilt. There was much to learn about being alive and alone as a widow.

After reading Jane Juska's account of her late-life adventures as a single woman in her book, *A RoundHeeled Woman,* I wondered about placing a personal ad. Juska bought one in the *New York Review of Books* stating she was looking to have sex before turning 67 in the next year. She got so many offers she had to triage them into piles before making selections. Not that

I wanted to be another round-heeled woman, but out of curiosity, I picked up a copy of *Washington Life* magazine to see what kind of guy might have posted a personal ad there. The writer described himself as a psychiatrist who was eager to meet a professional woman for "conversation and adventure." I answered the ad, and began a strange correspondence, exchanging pictures with him and trying to figure out how we could meet halfway between Houston, Texas and Virginia. I was planning a trip to Kentucky to visit Bob and Bobbi when they lived there and suggested we might meet in Louisville.

"Okay," he said on the phone. "I can stay with you in their guest room. You can trust me."

"Trust you to do something, or not?" I wondered. I hadn't invited him to meet Bob and Bobbi Damp. When I told Bobbi about his suggestion that I could "trust" him, her reaction was, "Let's forget about this one." I had to agree.

Careening about in the strange word of senior dating, life became a ride on bumper cars—more jolts and jounces, lumps and bumps, self-inflicted in my need to escape aloneness. At the time. I didn't realize such a quest would lead me to and through a number of experiences with varying degrees of cringe-value. On a scale of 1-10, I deemed a 10 as the most cringe-worthy

Cringe value: 7 out of 10

Garden Party Encounter

"You must meet Calvin," my friend Andrea announced.

"Oh yes! She must meet him," echoed another.

"He's grieving so much for his wife and wants to meet someone. He's quite well off, and drives a white Mercedes. An interesting person too."

The opportunity came one beautiful spring day at a garden tour with my mother; who came to visit her newly widowed daughter. My father had died two years before, and now I was joining her as a new widow, age 56. At 78, mother was old enough to expect to be a widow, but I felt too young to be one. What is this new role? I hadn't paid dues in this club, yet I was a member. I was confused. Where does a widow put her emotions?

As we walked away from a wine and cheese reception at the garden club, I noticed a dapper-looking fellow hurrying after us. He wore a well-tailored light blue suit complementing his head full of snow-white hair.

"Hello, I'm Calvin," he proffered. "I understand you lost your husband. How long ago?"

"Six months."

"It's been *six years* for me. It doesn't get any better."

Ignoring the portent of his observation, I replied, "My mother and I are on our way to finish the garden tour."

"Oh, are you going to the small garden on the next street? I'll see you there."

He arrived shortly after us and detained me by the delphiniums. His deluxe white Mercedes purred in the driveway behind him.

"Would you like to go to dinner with me after this?"

"Well, I'll have to ask my mother," I said, reverting to about thirteen.

"Bring her along," he said.

Guiding my mother into another corner of the garden, I told her, "Listen, this guy just asked me to dinner and I don't want to go. I'm going to tell him you don't want me to go."

Mom and I laughed all the way home at how I brushed him off. She clearly picked up on my amusement at using her as an excuse to get away from him. How thoughtless of him to tell me it wasn't "going to get any better." It felt good to have a giggle about it with my usually taciturn mother.

Later that evening, he found my number in the phonebook and called. First, he asked me about my husband.

"What did he do?" Then, "Do you have children? How old are they? What do they do?"

Soon it felt like an interview, but I bristled as he proceeded at length to describe his wonderful marriage.

"It was the best marriage anyone could have. And she was the best wife any man could ask for. We never argued about anything."

As the litany of praise for his late wife enlarged, I felt a certain rage building inside me and reached for a way to end this conversation.

"Listen, I simply can't deal with your issues now. I'm not able. Thank you for calling. Goodbye."

I flew into the other room where Mom was sitting in front of the television. She willingly became a silent sounding board for my rage and frustration: "Imagine. It seemed like I was being interviewed, asking me about my family, Mom. He asked how long we were married and about our children. Plus, he asked me where I went to school, but it was all a prelude to letting me know how perfect his marriage was. You and I know there is no such thing. He's just deluding himself so he can brag to unsuspecting widows. What kind of reaction was he expecting?"

Mother sat still, continuing her silent witness to my crackle, as my voice became louder and more frantic.

I loved her for not changing the subject this time. Uncharacteristically, she let it be all about me.

I rose in a fury, set off by this man's story. It was clear I was intensely, solidly deep into the anger phase of grief—one grieving widow who didn't want to hear more about this man's perfect, albeit, deceased wife. Furthermore, I didn't want to be interviewed for the vacancy. Mother watched me in uncertain silence as I stormed toward the door.

"I'm not that desperate to have to listen to him or have anything to do with him, even though he does drive a white Mercedes."

My black Thunderbird waited for me in the garage.

"I have to go out. I'm taking the car."

I drove into the black night until my fury abated, returning to the comfort of my own home, my mother's company and the memory of my own fine imperfect marriage.

Cringe value: 6 out of 10

The Editor

Part of my anger toward Calvin could have been frustration at not hearing from a man I had met in church the week before. I knew I made an impression on him because his ears turned red when he passed the offering plate to me. Maybe it was like Liz Taylor's affair with Eddie Fisher after Mike Todd died in a plane crash. I remember reading a magazine article quoting Liz: "He's dead. I'm alive."

After a couple of days, the man from church invited me to hear Mahler's Symphony No. 1 in the Virginia Beach Symphony Hall. Buoyed by the evening's sensual music, I said "Goodnight" but couldn't say "Goodbye." I threw my arms around him and took him to bed. As the old song goes, "Maybe I'm right, maybe I'm wrong; nevertheless, I'm in love with you."

I had been a widow for only a few months. We were not a good match, yet in the throes of a period of what Margaret Mead called "menopausal zest," my hormones were raging, and I was determined to have him. We began a three-year affair.

One morning I left him sleeping in my bed and went to work without waking him, since he had toiled until midnight the night before at the restaurant he ran in town. Later, my cleaning lady came in the house, and found him. The next time she saw me, there was a curious tone in her voice. "How are you?" she asked. "Great," I said. "But forgetful. I forgot to warn you someone would be in my house." She smiled. I didn't care.

When I told my mother about my new guy, she became alarmed. "He's only out for your money. You're making a big mistake."

I hadn't considered myself a rich widow, but this was the '90s. My investment funds were perking along and I had a full-time teaching salary. Still I was angered at her insinuation that it was my money that attracted him to me. Surely I had enough allure on my own. Mother's attitude was insulting. Looking back, I am still convinced he felt the same passion I did at first. It was a fling, but we both knew we weren't going to be married.

One summer day we returned to the house together to find a hummingbird flying under the cathedral ceiling. Immediately, I remembered my grandmother's old superstition: "A bird in the house is a sign of death."

While we watched, wondered how he got in, and what to do about it; the tiny creature collapsed on the carpeted stairs, his body heaving with exhaustion. How long had he been flying without food? Hummingbirds have the highest rate of metabolism of any animal—roughly 100 times that of an elephant. We had to do something quickly. I approached the gasping creature carefully, placed him into a pillowcase, carried him to the back porch and gave him to my lover. After I fixed some sugar water, we held a spoon under his tiny beak and he drank. Then he rested a bit. Suddenly, he rose up and flew away, restored to flight and life. It was tempting to think this hummingbird was the embodiment of Jim's spirit, using it to give us his blessing for our affair only four months after his death.

My lover was a big help editing the papers I was writing for my doctoral work. After he noted the typos and tense disagreements, I would ask, "What did you think of it?"

Each time, he admitted, "Oh, I didn't understand any of it."

Three years had slipped by and neither our minds nor the lovemaking were in harmony. Even so, I was reluctant to end it. Perhaps I just needed to have someone breathing in the next room as I managed to balance my full-time work with the demands of a doctoral program.

As my world was expanding with new ideas, he seemed to have no interest in my efforts. He wasn't very handy in the sense of fixing things, but handy to have around because each month when I left for weekend seminars in Alexandria, he house-sat for me and developed a charming relationship with my cat, Sadie.

No words of true love were uttered even in our most intimate moments and I began to feel him pulling away as well. The affair was cooling off, like Ella Fitzgerald sang,

So, good-bye, dear, and amen
Here's hoping we meet now and then
It was great fun
But it was just one of those things
If we'd thought a bit, of the end of it
When we started painting the town We'd have been aware that our love affair Was too hot, not to cool down.

One weekend while I had been away at class, and he was taking care of my cat and house-sitting, he left a note saying, "Put a fork in it."

Isn't that what one does to see if a baked potato is done? He had met an old schoolmate, now a divorcee, at a party. Within a year, they were married.

I should give him credit for some virtue. Instead of cheating on me, he broke it off. Though I knew our relationship had been foundering for some time, this was a rejection that bruised and I shed angry tears. What was it that made me unwilling to give it up? The Cinderella

Complex—fear of being utterly alone, perhaps. But there it was. I had to face the fact—I was alone with the cat.

Cringe value: 5 out of 10

Dancing Stork

His personal ad sounded great. He described himself as tall, with a great sense of humor. He sounded agreeable, so I met him at a diner for lunch. Pulling into the parking lot next to the gray car he described, I noticed his profile in the driver's seat. It was a small, almost hairless round head featuring a prominent nose that pointed down to an even more prominent mouth under which there was very little chin. The similarity to a stork was complete when he unfolded his great height from the seat and stood up to greet me. He was pale, with wisps of white hair and vivid blue eyes that matched his polo shirt.

Lumbering ahead of me up the few steps to the door, his long legs seemed connected under his armpits. Our menus were in hand as he told me, "You should know right away I'm not interested in getting married."

He doesn't want to get married. Ha! As if I'd ever consider marrying him.

Instead of standing up and exclaiming, *"Well, that did it."* and walking away, I studied the menu.

During the Caesar salad, I learned about his smart successful son and looked at a picture of his grandson. But most of the conversation was about how he went to visit his aged mother in the nursing home every day and was truly devoted to her. My mother was also in a nursing home then, but we never got around to talking about how she stopped eating and was being kept alive with a feeding tube. So far, there was little evidence of his reported sense of humor unless he was trying to be funny about not getting married.

Returning to our cars, he asked if I'd like to go dancing sometime. I tried to imagine dancing with this storky guy, but gamely answered,

"I'll have to get some proper dancing shoes."

"I'll call you," he said as he folded himself behind the steering wheel. I couldn't wait to drive away. Pulling onto the highway, a wave of grief combined with anger toward Jim hit me.

Why did you leave me in this mess, my handsome charismatic husband? We were just getting our marriage right. We had more to do. It was a too-short 29 years. Why did you leave me alone here in this swamp? You were never even sick! I found you, still warm, face-down on the floor. No warning, except for the pain in your neck I massaged the night before. Why? Why?

I sped away as fast as I could legally go, tears streaming down my face.

In a few days, the Stork called, "Miriam, Mother died last night, but in our last conversation I told her I met a woman who had the same first name as her sister. That made her so happy. She said it was wonderful I met you."

"I'm so sorry. You must be very sad."

"Oh yes," he said. "But I have to make the funeral arrangements now. Call me."

I never did. Grief can be a solitary thing.

Cringe value: 4 out of 10

Skating Motorcycle Guy

After the turn of the century, my adventures were limited to working, choral singing, travel and summer trips to Chautauqua Institution, which bills itself as a "Festival of Mind, Body and Spirit." I love its Victorian charm and bucolic location in the rolling hills of western New York State.

I met a friend, Carol Hicks, in a popular café and she introduced me to another woman friend. We were having an introductory chat about where we were from when a man sitting alone at the next table interrupted. He had been listening to our conversation.

"You're from Albany?" he asked me.

"I worked there until I retired from the state."

I was startled to see he was wearing inline roller skates, making him appear quite elongated as he lounged in his chair, legs stretched out.

"Really? My mother retired from the state too."

"What was her name?"

"Ruth Sanderson"

"You knew my mother?"

"I have many stories about your mother."

Now he had my full attention while the women at my table started a conversation of their own.

She was the District AO," he said, adding that he was "intertwined" with her for many years.

"Everyone respected her," he said. "She had her principles and she stuck to them, no matter what the pressures were. She didn't get along with everybody, but I always thought she was in the right."

His description of Mother's office location in downtown Albany where she had spent over 30 years convinced me he really knew her. He looked at his watch. "Hey, I've got to go."

I was trying to imagine the point of view of a man who had worked with her. How did she appear to others who knew her only professionally? And what were those stories?

"I'd like to hear more about my mother's office days. She's gone now. She died last year."

"Okay, I'll call you," he assured me as he rose to an impressive height and skated out of the café. His call came later, proposing that we go to lunch the next day and would I mind if we went on his motorcycle?

This guy was full of surprises.

When he pulled up and offered me a helmet, I sang, "I don't want a pickle, I just want to ride on your motorcycle."

"A pickle?" he asked. (He didn't get my playful rendering of the Arlo Guthrie song.)

We sped off down the road. This was only my second ride on the back of a motorcycle; I held on tight to his jacket. The sun was streaming down on us. I felt like a teenager.

Arriving at the restaurant, we sat on a bench in the sun. Had I plucked out all stray hairs on my chin? Putting on my sunglasses, I looked him over through dark lenses. He was lean and obviously fit, with a few traces of gray in his straight blond hair.

The conversation turned to his estranged wife.

"She's dangerous, so I can't live with her."

"Dangerous?"

"She starts fires."

"How's that?"

"She drinks and then falls asleep with a lit cigarette."

He continued, "I've tried to help her, but I can't. She is the one with the problem, and she's got to do something about it."

The full impact of his situation was revealed when he noted his friends said he wasn't capable of making a commitment with any other woman because he was still so involved with his wife.

That was certainly true. Riding back on the motorcycle, he kept talking about his wife. I pried in his ear, "It sounds like the relationship is in flux."

"Maybe. I don't know," he said.

His friends were right. He wasn't ready for a commitment, and neither was I. As he sped off on his motorcycle, I realized he hadn't told me anything more about my mother. I believed he was right about having worked for her and his name was familiar, but he hadn't shared any of those stories he mentioned earlier. Apparently, there were more compelling issues on his mind, leaving me with another short bumper-car encounter.

Cringe value: 5 out of 10

The Vegetarian

It's tricky to be with a vegan whose life is ruled by convictions against society's wasteful, earth-adverse habits. We met at a singles club event. He was tall and wore a plaid shirt over his broad shoulders. It was easy to dismiss his annoyance at finding coffee served in Styrofoam coffee cups, but then I learned he avoided waste in other ways by biking to work in all seasons and weather. Before the show, we could choose between a vegetarian meal and filet mignon. I chose the beef. When I left a thick piece of meat, he pointed to my plate.

"Are you going to finish that?"

"No, it's too much for me."

He picked it up with his fork, put it in his mouth, chewed and swallowed it.

"I thought you didn't eat meat."

"I don't, but that creature died so you could eat. It shouldn't be wasted."

From there, we had little else to talk about. I was obviously too uncouth and wasteful for his regard. We didn't bother to exchange phone numbers. He was 50 and unmarried, probably still single, unless he found someone else as devoted to saving the earth and treating its creatures properly. I'm just a contributor to wildlife charities like save the whales and polar bears. He took a stand at every turn. To him, I was just another meat eater. However, I learned never to order steak while dining with a vegetarian.

Hold on, that bump was easier.

Cringe value: 3 out of 10

Schooner Man

The Mystic Whaler was waiting at the dock. This three-day Elderhostel program (the Baby Boomers changed the name to Road Scholars) was sailing from Mystic Connecticut on Long Island Sound in a reproduction of a 19th century coastal cargo schooner. It seemed like a perfect getaway for a widow spreading her wings and looking for a little adventure.

Crowding onto the deck, I was jostled into the fellow in front of me.

"Oh, excuse me," I said.

He turned, and taking my measure, "That's okay; do it again." We were in a playful mood. During the group orientation, we eyed each other. There were several single women and apparently one single man. The rest appeared to be older married couples in the prime of retirement.

The captain introduced us to a sea-chantey singer whose voice rang out on the river as we made our way out of the harbor and onto the Long Island Sound. He taught us to sing chanteys while pulling the ropes rhythmically to raise the schooner's bountiful sails. Soon, we were underway before the wind.

My roommate and I found our tiny bunks in the hold of the ship. We had triangular bunk beds tucked under the prow, barely enough room for one of us to stand up in the space between the beds and the wall while dressing and undressing.

Each morning, noon and night, wonderful meals emanated from the tiny mess, served buffet-style on the deck benches and sea chests. We listened to lectures about all things nautical, from anchors and whales to life as a whaling captain's wife told by our captain's wife dressed in a period costume. We also docked for tours of historic sites along the shoreline. Evenings were spent under the stars, anchored in safe harbors whose waters gently lapped against the ship.

We single women were curious about the one single fellow in our midst. Schooner Man appeared to be in his mid-50s, sturdily built, and not much taller than I. What was his story? We learned that he was a retired pathologist who had built his own home in Pennsylvania's Pocono Mountains. I noticed that he stashed a bottle of liquor in one of the sea chests where beverages were kept. One late morning as a fresh breeze whipped the sails and snapped the ropes, I caught him having a nip and he winked at me.

Like a bee in a flower garden, he would distribute his favors by sitting next to each of us in turn. I noted in my journal: "D— is a real rake, continuing to make subtle passes. He doesn't smile easily except at his own mischievous comments."

On one encounter, I pried, "So, are you married?"

"No."

"Ever come close?"

"No."

There was no sense continuing my inquisition with this one.

On the final night, we crowded together on the benches after dinner, enjoying the night air and companionship. Suddenly, Schooner Man slid onto a small space on the bench next to me. He leaned in and to my deep and everlasting astonishment, whispered in my ear: "We're never going to see each other again, so how about some oral sex?"

If I did have something clever to say, I was sure the woman so close on the other side of me would hear it.

Gape-mouthed at first, I managed to whisper: "What?"

He repeated it.

I mumbled out of the corner of my mouth, "Who do you think I am?"

My ego was really bruised and my thoughts raced.

You crummy warped bastard. I'm certainly not interested in seeing you again, and here you are asking me to have some kind of oral sex in a public place. Where do you think we'd do the dirty? Under the gunnels? Or maybe we can push our roommates out the door? It may be dark, but oh God, there's a woman sitting right next to me here who could be listening to this.

Leaping to my feet, I escaped to the lower deck where I picked up my guitar, and found a group to lead some singing. Schooner Man appeared in the doorway and stood for a while, glaring at me. I ignored him, glad when he finally disappeared.

In the morning, I caught up with him as we left the schooner.

"I want to ask you something. Do you remember what you asked me last night?"

"Did you think I was so drunk I don't remember? It's just that I am taking blood-pressure medicine and I can't take Viagra."

It was a hell of an explanation.

Cringe value: 10 out of 10

The Canadian

The Amtrak train was crowded on the trip home from New York City. Instead of settling down in my riverside window seat to enjoy the scenery, I joined the line at the café car. A jolly light-haired fellow in a blue T-shirt offered me a place in line.

"You stand right here," he suggested with a charming Scots-Canadian brogue, "and then you can sit at our table," to which he pointed.

I obeyed his forceful suggestion and took my place with him and others at the table. The conversation centered on what we knew about the history of the Hudson River. Two docents in the cafe provided guides to the riparian views of the lighthouses, memorial sentinels of past river commerce, as well as interesting tidbits about the ruins of Bannerman's castle arsenal off the eastern shore.

The Canadian was animated and easy to talk to, a journalist who soon turned the conversation to U.S. politics. I took great pains to explain I was not to blame for Bush's mess in Iraq because I was a liberal Democrat. We both got off at the Albany-Rensselaer station where the train changed engines before continuing to Montreal. He found me on the platform and asked for my email before re-boarding.

The hounding began with emails asking me to visit him in Vermont or join him on one of his visits to New York City. I agreed to meet him for lunch and chose a pretty day in the fall to drive to Burlington. We met in a card shop.

"Hi,s" I said as he came in the door. "This is crazy."

"Yes, it is," he agreed. "My car is parked outside."

We drove to a diner that was warm and clean, and took a booth.

His first topic was not a good omen. "I had a heart attack; it just happened this week. I don't know how serious it is yet, but I'm taking medications. It's been a frightening experience."

"What brings you to Burlington today?"

"My wife is at a conference. It's just a few blocks away at the college." He had been vague about his marital status in our emails. This revelation dampened my mood.

His mood had changed as well. He was no longer the cheerful spirit I met on the train and I started to imagine what his wife had gone through during the past week. As we spooned our soup, the conversation stayed focused on his health.

"I play soccer every week. I thought I was healthy. I had no idea this was coming."

"What did the doctors recommend?"

"I see a specialist next week. Meanwhile, I'm on blood pressure meds."

When the check came, he asked, "Do you mind paying the bill? I would pay, but I don't have American dollars, just Canadian currency."

"Sure," I said, handing over a 20-dollar bill, wondering why he wasn't better prepared for our meeting.

He suggested we go to a small local museum. There, in a dark deserted corner, he came onto me with hot breath and roaming hands. I pushed him away gently, forcing a smile with visions of his inopportune demise.

I wasn't encouraging him after that encounter, but he persisted. His emails kept coming with overtures to meet him under the clock at Grand Central and other romantic places.

"I owe you lunch," he wrote.

I considered that debt erased.

Cringe value: 7 out of 10 minus $20

The Conservative

"Ask me how I lost five pounds last weekend," I gurgled to a friend. "I went to a singles dance and met a man who is a great dancer. What's more, he's a pilot; he sails and even roller skates."

At least, that's what he told me. When he asked me to dance, he smiled and I noticed his beautiful white teeth. We danced together the rest of the night. He escorted me to my car and asked if he could take me to dinner and dancing the next evening. I was charmed and asked if he was around my age, telling him I was 64, and he nodded with that beautiful smile. I thought he might be a candidate for a serious relationship.

After several daily phone calls, and another date with dinner and dancing, I whirled away with my fantasies about this man, searching for poetry about love and smiles. We would marry. I started to plan the wedding, fantasizing about a location, even the guest list. One evening as we pulled into a parking lot before attending an evening service at his church, we discussed another couple.

"They're going to get married too," I blurted out.

"Are you asking me to marry you?"

"Maybe."

As we sat close together during the service, I realized this was a "praise" church. I'd spent the better part of my adult life as a traditional Presbyterian, and felt uncomfortable with this kind of worship music. Perhaps unreasonably, anything short of pipe organ accompaniment to traditional church music was anathema to me. In this church, the minister wore jeans and people played guitars accompanied by snare drums. The congregation stood up and waved their hands about to lift their prayers to heaven.

Warning bells replaced wedding bells as I began to realize I might be making a mistake. After the service, my dancing man introduced me around to his spiritual partners and leaders. I grew worried and felt out of place.

Alone at my house, we kissed and shortly, we were on my bed where we had unmemorable sex. He soon left with that wonderful smile on his face.

On our next date, he said he had something serious to discuss with me. Stretching out his long thin legs on my couch he said, "I think I should tell my daughter we had sex."

"Why on earth would you do that? Parents don't tell their children about their sex lives."

"Well, all right, but I think I should."

"Don't be silly."

"Really, our children don't want to know. It's our business only."

How could he be serious?

Doubting my own mind, the first attraction was fading, along with the memory of the dancing. He made plans to cook a lobster dinner at his home the following weekend. I was to bring my toothbrush and stay the night. Before dinner, he pointed out a small, sad, dilapidated sailboat parked behind his garage.

That boat will never sail again. I thought. *Remembering now that he had told me about being in the merchant marines on Liberty Ships during World War II, I was afraid to do the math. How old was he?*

In the cluttered basement of his small ranch house, he told me he had plans to move down there and rent out the rest of the house. I almost said, "How depressing!" In the bedroom, I found the only reading material in the house: copies of the National Review on the nightstand along with Freedom magazine, a rag of the NRA. My fantasies were fading fast.

I decided to make up an excuse to go home. Before I left, he kissed me so hard he bit my lip. Through the pain, I realized those pearlies were false—a beautiful false-toothed smile.

On our next date, he confessed he was planning to have a face lift because he thought he was having trouble getting dates. I didn't think he needed it, after all I was still dating him, but he was determined.

A few weeks later, his daughter called to say he had come out of the anesthesia, but had to go back to the recovery room because, as she put it, "he had a little stroke." She said he had a phone in his room and would I call and pick him up at the hospital to drive him home? When he answered the phone, I asked for directions to his room, but he had great difficulty responding and seemed quite confused. I found a frail old man whose head was swathed in bandages. Only his mouth and bruised eyes were visible.

On the way home, he asked me to stop at a pharmacy to fill his pain prescription. The pharmacist asked me if the patient was born in 1923. I nodded with a slack jaw. Now I was forced to do the math in earnest. That meant the man sitting in my car was 78 and in very bad shape. This was not the time to challenge him. It looked like his roller-skating days were over as he staggered up the ramp to his house.

In the days following, our phone conversations were starting to irritate me because he seemed so amused at my liberal leanings. Patiently, with some measure of condescension, he explained how gun control limited the Second Amendment. I was tired of defending my strong political convictions, saying, "I can't do this" and cut the conversation short.

For months afterward, I would hear his messages left on my answering machine, telling me how much he liked talking to a "liberal young lady." I wasn't answering. Without a doubt, this conservative, fundamentalist who enjoyed condescending to my views and wanted to tell his daughter about his sex life wasn't the guy for me. I was beginning to regret the "finding someone" mode. As Shakespeare observed, "What fools these mortals be."

Cringe value: 10 out of 10.

Internet Dating

A friend recommended Concerned Singles online as a good place to start internet dating. The website described itself as a place to meet others "who share your progressive values and are in sync with your philosophical and political outlook." It seemed made to order for someone with my left-of-center leanings.

After posting my profile, I received a letter in the mail from a gentleman who appeared to be recruiting volunteers to join his church group for a summer in Ghana. I really couldn't imagine myself working on a water development project in my own backyard, let alone in Africa. Blessings on him and those in his group, but my idea of a trip to Africa would be something like having Robert Redford fly me over the savanna toward the sunset, not digging wells.

Trying to sort out the strange from the simply conceited, I read another post on the dating site: *This guitar-playing charmer has it all–looks, musical talent and a romantic side! A hopeless romantic at heart, he loves everything from walking hand in hand under the moonlight to soft kisses wrapped in laughter and blushing.*

Somehow, that one didn't move me to act. Was I no longer a romantic?

I also resisted: *Sensitive, caring man who is personable, romantic, and affectionate.* Or consider this one: *Looking for a travel and activity friend.*

Another one wrote an intriguing self-description to go with his boasting ID: *"Likes dogs, old motorcycles, travel, very easy going. Looking for someone to share same."* His picture showed a large man with an enormous gray beard. Uncombed, wild hair framed his round face; chubby cheeks completed his disheveled Santa Claus image.

That description might appeal to many a lonely woman, but most of these descriptions are deceiving.With internet dating, I would select a likely candidate to contact via email after viewing his self-descriptions and pictures; then after some email exchanges, we spoke on the phone. During one conversation, the fellow questioned me about my height and weight, asking if I'd be willing to lose 15 pounds. Obviously, this egotist thought he deserved someone more physically fit. Whatever my charms might have been, my weight held sway.

Another internet contact was a divorced professor with a history of several marriages resulting in a total of six children. He complained, "When I meet these women in person, they don't look as young as the pictures they post on the dating site." He, however, looked very much like himself in his picture—a stocky man with a ruddy complexion. We dated a couple of times. In spite of our common interests, I told him I wasn't interested in sex. Soon after, he informed me he had met a younger woman online who was a rich divorcee and thought he was a real stud. I guess this was some kind of retribution for telling him I was just looking for a companion, but I didn't care. Anyway, his brutal honesty belied an overblown opinion of himself.

One swarthy fellow peered at me under heavy gray brows and through thick-rimmed lenses.

"Do you always wear glasses?" he asked.

"Yes," I explained, "I can see without them, but the details of my food are clearer when I wear them."

I crossed out that guy, then dated another who claimed to be a poet who shared some rather unimpressive verses with me. It felt like I had become an interviewer as well as an interviewee who wasn't really interested in the job. All I really wanted was a nice dinner date and interesting conversation, so I returned to my internet dating search.

Cringe value: 3 out of 10

Garlic Man

His posting on the Concerned Singles website indicated that he was literate and passionate about liberal causes. I was pleased he didn't ask about my weight when we spoke on the phone. In addition, he lived in an interesting town in the Berkshires, close to my brother's home. After a brief conversation, we made plans to meet and he gave me his address. I asked my brother to investigate.

"Miriam, he has puppets on his front porch."

"What do you mean, puppets?"

"Well, they're really mannequins, dressed up and standing there."

"And he has a little box in his front yard, like the ones they put out to sell a house. His picture is on it and a bio, saying he's looking for a woman."

"That sounds a bit kooky, but I've decided to meet him anyway. He wants to take me to a concert and dinner in the evening and a museum the next day."

Why did I decide to go ahead with the date after hearing about this guy's strange bid for female company? What should I do, call him and say, "Thanks for the invitation, but I heard you have some kind of puppets in your front yard?"

That would have been too much honesty. I would have had to make up a lie—a small lie, but it would be hard to do without him suspecting I was creating an excuse. No, maybe this wasn't so weird, maybe this guy is fun to be with.

I met him at my brother's house.

He was a slight man with a halo of curly gray hair atop a freckled face—a pleasant, smiling elf. The boys' school chapel was a lovely setting for a summer concert featuring a soprano and cellist. We settled in the crowd, and as the hall warmed up, I noticed a strong smell of garlic emanating from my date. As the evening progressed, I was trapped in a haze of garlic-laden air. The music soared, and so did the garlic. I longed for the intermission and a chance to get outside. When it came, I filled my lungs with cool mountain air before we returned for the rest of the program.

Garlic followed me into the car, and into the restaurant where I learned he had actually been a rocket scientist and worked for NASA. Still, I couldn't bring myself to ask him about the puppets on his porch. However, he did share something else about his interest in women. His face took on a wanly delighted look. "I decided to find a woman after I had a delightful relationship one evening with a young lady," he said.

"She made me realize I was physically capable."

This news did not appeal to me at all. I soon managed to ask if he had certain dietary habits; perhaps he regularly ate some particular food?

"No, not at all."

Back in the car, I tried to imagine spending another minute breathing his air.

At my brother's house, with door knob in my hand, escape was near.

"What time should I pick you up tomorrow to go to the museum?"

"Uuuh, I'm not really interested in doing that now. Thanks for a lovely evening." I turned the knob, stepping briskly inside, breathing deeply, happy to have my own air.

Cringe value: 8 out of 10 (Sorry, try again)

Boat Man

He had a new boat and was sailing up the Hudson to the Champlain Canal, planning to dock overnight near my home. On our internet chat, he explained he had real estate properties in Manhattan that were "doing well." The extent of his kind of ownership didn't really sink in until I met him where he docked his boat. I was late coming from a meeting with a client and found him pacing in the parking lot. He was tall and thin, and his long face looked familiar.

During dinner, we soon discovered that Jim had taught his children to swim at a Westchester country club. I remembered spending an evening on his yacht years ago when Jim and I were invited to for an evening sail on Long Island Sound. As we uncovered more revelations about the past, he seemed to recoil from me.

After dinner, we walked back to the waterfront and I suggested a tour of Albany across the river.

He demurred, "I've been there; I'm invited for drinks at the yacht docked in front of my boat."

Boat man got out of my car and bid me a quick goodbye. Maybe he was still annoyed about my lateness.

No country club life for me.

Cringe value: 2 out of 10

Sewer Man and Dog

Still searching for a meaningful relationship online, and unsure of my future, I thought this might be the one I was looking for. In person, he resembled the picture on his profile—a broad smile in a round face topped by a full head of snow-white hair. He was slightly stooped over his paunch, causing the back of his sport coat to rise higher than the front.

We had been waiting to meet in person since we began an intense period of email correspondence. He provided a long resume listing his successful life in water management, dealing with the important aspects of keeping sewers functioning properly.

He started perusing the online dating site after a serious fall causing broken bones in his foot. We had been corresponding for two months when his doctor finally gave him permission to drive.

"Come in, come in and see how my foot has healed." He beckoned me into his motel room and sat on the edge of the bed, removing his foot cast and sock, exposing a still swollen ankle. The skin was pocked and scaly. I didn't want to see any more, and my appetite waned.

As quickly as I could, I suggested we be on our way to dinner. I had reservations in a chic restaurant where young people spilled out into the restaurant's terrace, dancing to loud music.

"No, not this place," he said. "Just something simple —like Applebee's."

So, I drove on to another restaurant that looked more upscale than Applebee's; it too was full.

Between emails over the past three months, there had been numerous phone calls. Each time he assured me he never lost his temper. He spoke with an accent reflecting his origins in the Middle East, relating what a good life he had created for his wife and two sons before his impending divorce. His wife had left him and was living in England.

"Strange your wife took off. Do you have an explanation you could share? Surely it wasn't your terrible temper," I observed in an attempt at humor.

"We do not know for sure. She didn't share with anyone. She didn't demand anything and refused counseling. An old male friend is involved."

I pressed for more information about this woman who slipped out of his life after a long marriage.

"What was she like?"

"She was a wonderful housekeeper and she liked to knit. I don't understand why she left."

"It was a delightful one hour and forty minutes," he wrote after a phone call. "On the one hand I am flying high with the expectation of meeting you in person; on the other hand, I am dead worried that I do not deserve you. You are such a sweet person."

"I fear you may be disappointed" I wrote back. "I'm best seen in dim light these days."

I told him about my life: my work, my great second-life career, my sons and their careers, my choral singing and my blonde cocker spaniel, Casey. (I was as silly about Casey as only a dog owner can understand.)

"How do you feel about dogs?" I asked.

He returned with a non-answer: "No comment about Casey."

That non-comment faded when a huge floral arrangement arrived at my door. It was so large, it would have been perfect for a funeral, but it graced my living room table for weeks. Every time I looked at it, I thought to myself, "This guy's generous."

Then he administered the *coup de gras*, writing, "You are working nearly full time. Time to slow down?" Cinderella visions began—someone who would take care of me in my advancing years—a more leisurely life with fewer financial worries and maybe a chance to travel. In spite of some concerns about what other ailments a man 72-year-old might be facing, I wondered, *Did I really want to give up my independence?* I was about to have a glimpse of what it would be like.

Now we had finally met in person and I was driving him through the night as my visions of a dinner in a nice place (not Applebee's) started to fade. Finally, I found a rather grubby Chinese restaurant that met his approval. I ordered plum wine; it wasn't the icy cool Cosmopolitan cocktail I had envisioned. I wondered what to do about the next day, which coincidentally was his birthday. I feared I would disappoint this man who seemed so pleased with himself for finding me. The next morning, I was preparing a breakfast for him when he arrived, but he had already eaten.

"The motel had a free continental breakfast, and I ate there." He spoke with the satisfaction of someone who watches his pennies.

I leaned over to pet Casey's curly top. He watched and asked: "How old is this dog?" Followed by, "How long do those dogs live?"

I responded cautiously, "About 12 or 13 years. Why?"

"I'll have to wait another six or seven for you."

"How about waiting until never," I thought.

I settled on the couch and he took the easy chair. I turned on the TV for some distraction and actually began to nod off after hearing again about how he always took his family on a camping vacation. My head snapped back quickly when I realized he had rolled onto the couch and had surrounded me with his paunchy self. It was like being kissed by the Pillsbury dough boy.

I pulled myself out of the pillow dough and sat on a chair.

"I can't do this."

"Why? What's wrong?"

"It's me, not you," I lied. "I'm just turned off and don't want to be touched."

"Not by you," is what I really meant.

Lying again, "It's a problem I have."

"You must have a problem. Maybe you should see a counselor, get some help."

123

"Yes, I should, you're right. Meanwhile, I'm exhausted. I haven't slept all night."

"I should leave. I will leave and I will go home and teach bridge classes and meet other people."

"Good for you."

Closing the door behind him, I was filled with monumental relief. I twirled around with joy to be out from the specter of attaching myself to this dog-hating bore. How could I get myself into a situation where I had to lie and demean myself to get out of it?

Letting go of the leisure life fantasy and happily taking Casey's leash, we set off onto the rest of our life together. This one made me wake up. I hated internet dating. *Enough bumps and bruises; I'm getting off this ride now*, I thought. My life on bumper car ride dates was a useful learning experience, teaching me to value the smooth road where relative peace and happiness is found.

At last, I was out of the amusement park, laughing at myself. Sometimes all a gal needs is a fuzzy dog at the end of a leash.

Cringe value: 10 out of 10

Chapter IV
Off to See the World

Nobody said not to go.

Emily Hahn

An Alto Travels

My voice teacher and dear friend, Dr. Virginia Davidson, phoned, "My group is going to Finland and Russia. You should join us; we can use your voice," she said.

Virginia came into my life when I was the principal's wife in Saranac Lake. She was part of the Adirondack Vocal/Choral summer workshop with the late Gregg Smith, composer and director of the eponymous Gregg Smith Singers. I was a soprano then, and began studying voice with Gregg's wife, Roz Rees, an accomplished professional soprano. Jim and I became their friends, often visiting their camp on the Saranac River, which, in honor of their terriers, they named Barkhaven. Once, after hearing a performance of one of

Gregg's compositions, Jim observed: "The hairs on the back of my neck stood up." Later, Gregg gave Jim a copy with those words set to music. Both Jim and Gregg shared birthdays in August which we celebrated at Barkhaven, drinking wine and telling musical stories until it was time to follow the Saranac River back to town—a magical fifteen-minute boat ride through the foggy night.

In my newly widowed state, I often drove to the city to stay with Virginia in her Upper West Side apartment as one of countless singers she sheltered, nourished, taught and inspired. Once she introduced me to her professional singers group, saying, "Miriam has such a beautiful voice." I basked in her high praise, knowing in spite of my lost high soprano notes, I was able to use strength in the lower register. We both knew my musicality was lacking, never good enough to become a professional, however, under her direction, I flourished as a low alto where I could supply a solid depth to the group's sound. In my new identity as a Davidson singer alto, I developed an appreciation of what life offered in my new identity as a Davidson singer alto. Amidst the rubble of my life, traveling with Virginia's group gave me much to look forward to and at times the only certainty I could find.

The Davidson Singers were twelve men and women, lifelong singers with one thing in common: we enjoyed performing under Virginia's skilled direction. Most of us had studied voice individually with her and prior to our tours, we rehearsed together every week for months in her studio apartment.

We learned important life lessons as well: be on time for rehearsals, use a pencil to take notes, listen to others, breathe deeply, watch the director, come in on time, sit and stand up straight and tune to the right pitch; wear clean black shoes and smile at applause. Also, I knew that it's ok to make mistakes because if you don't ever make one, it means you're probably not singing loud enough.

Unlike other art forms, music is ephemeral. Once you've performed it, it's gone, only to be appreciated in the movement of time. It's a shudder in the spine — a glimpse of the divine. The best part is to enter into the oneness of the music. Singing with the Davidson Singers, Gregg Smith Singers, or one of the larger groups I later joined, I would experience visceral sensations, breathing a series of vibrations into space along with the other voices, as we transformed black notes into the music of the ages. Yes, those cosmic smiles on choristers faces hint at the drugless high they feel.

While sheltered in the ensemble, my new life as a solo act began. My doctoral work was finished and I was still searching for an encore career. Meanwhile, I relished getting back to performing great choral music again with a new voice.

Places We Sang

The mission of the Davidson Singers' tours was to bring American choral music abroad, however, our repertoire of secular and sacred selections depended on the venue. We sang a Sunday morning Episcopal service on a steaming July Sunday in Athens; the next year on a tour of Mexico from the balcony of an Episcopal church in San Miguel de Allende, helping to celebrate the ordination of a Mexican bishop. In Germany, we not only sang a part of the morning mass in the great Cologne Cathedral, but later on the top deck of a tourist boat on the Rhine, we sang impromptu choruses of the *Lorelei*. Our version of the ballad in our American-accented German provided surprise entertainment as we floated past the rock in the middle of the river with the statue of the Loreli water spirits famed for luring sailors to their deaths. We rendered the American folk song, "Shenandoah" in a ruined castle in Heidelberg, where at least a couple of American Air Force officers stopped to listen. In Greece, just to hear our own echo, we sang

Gregg Smith's arrangement of "Blow the Candle Out" in Agamemnon's dry beehive-shaped tomb, just to hear ourselves singing an enticing American folk song:

Roll me in your arms love,
And blow the candle out.

Later that same day, we intoned a rousing "Rose of Sharon" from the Bible's Song of Solomon in the middle of the enormous Epidaurus amphitheater in the Peloponnese.

The basses shine in this piece when they start:

Rise up my fair one and come away,
For Lo the winter is past,

Then joined by the women:

The Rain is over and gone,
The rain is over, the rain is over, the rain is over and
gone.

Each venue has a different feeling. Some places have no resonance; others, like cathedrals, are too lively; but the amphitheater at Epidaurus was strangely invigorating. We took turns running to the top of the ancient rows of stone benches to listen. It was truly easy to hear every word clearly sung by our singers, little specks singing so far away down in the vast, ancient space.

In Scotland, we performed in the Highlands and the Lowlands, with stops to visit castles and Loch Ness (alas, no Nessie). I had a solo—an obscure Scottish lullaby, which Virginia arranged for soloist and chorus. After a concert in Inverness, we visited the Scottish Folk Music Museum Cafe, where people were invited to sing solos when the spirit moved them. After a glass of single malt courage, I took the small stage, and offered my lullaby *a cappella*. During that tour, all it took was a poke in the middle like one of those singing stuffed animals, and I'd render my "Baloo Lammy" solo part.

The National Museum in Edinburgh had many old masters, but my favorite was Frederic Church's "Niagara Falls." The huge painting was so magnificent one could almost feel the spray of the falls coming from the oil canvas.

As an American tourist in Europe and Mexico, sometimes I felt like a witness to a great crime. Shepherded around Rococo and Baroque cathedrals crowded with decorative art, where cherubs hung about in all corners, we walked on tightly formed mosaic flooring flecked with gold. The stained-glass windows might move some to tears when the sun shines through from on high, but not me. I recognize how the value and beauty of public architecture adds to our spiritual and cultural aesthetics, but wonder about the societies that spent so much gold on those buildings. For me, the thought of all that wealth spent on churches makes me resent how the rulers hogged the wealth while the people lived in poverty.

In a chapel of one such overwrought cathedral on our Mexican tour, we looked down at a mirror in the floor. It reflected an otherworldly white dove pictured in a little golden dome in the ceiling. Surrounded by its own cherubs, it seemed the most extreme example of this type of wretched excess, both beautiful and disquieting. Nonetheless, I looked forward to more opportunities to sing with Virginia's Davidson Singers in these amazing places.

Midnight Train to Moscow

In the summer of 1998, after a couple of days performing in Finland, The Davidson Singers boarded the night train from Helsinki to Moscow. It rolled nonstop, rails clicking, jostling me in and out of sleep on the top bunk. When morning finally arrived, bleak flat Russian fields streamed by our small compartment window. I swung my legs and feet to the sticky floor and dressed quickly in search of my traveling companions and most important, coffee.

If it had been a rough night for me, it must have been worse for the two guys slumped in the first booth of the cafe car. One had collapsed asleep on his guitar; the other listlessly dragged on a cigarette.

My friends were seated further away—the only others in the car, and they had coffee. Joining them, I looked around. Sheer pink curtains jiggled on the windows and small red lampshades on each table were more like a brothel than a railway car. When the smoking waiter stood up and reached for the coffee pot, I assumed he would soon offer me some. Catching his eye, I pointed hopefully at my cup on the table and then to myself. He returned a sideways sneer while pouring a cup, sat back down with it, and lit another cigarette from the first one. No coffee for me.

The Russians were having a hard time transitioning to capitalism and the concept of customer service. The old hotel in St. Petersburg allotted only one old-fashioned three-inch-long metal key to a room. My roommate and I liked the convenience of separate keys, so I gingerly approached the desk clerk.

"Could we please have two keys for our room?"

"One key—ONE key," he barked from behind a grated window.

Chastened, my roommate and I took the creaky elevator to the third floor, which, like all the hotel's floors installed a woman at a desk as a hall monitor for the purpose of keeping our key whenever we left our room.

Tour buses left promptly at 9 a.m., but we couldn't get needed rubles because the currency exchange did not open until 9:30. That tardy government service must have deprived the Russian economy of a significant amount of foreign currency each day by opening after the hotel emptied of tourists.

In the streets and parks, our dollars were actually preferred. Citizens were selling personal items they carried with them. I bought a Russian Army hat for my son—the kind that folds flat, complete with pins and medals.

I wore the hat while listening as our guide explained where Czar Nicholas and his family had recently been interred within the Church of Peter and Paul. After a few minutes, a young man, previously unnoticed, handed me a rolled paper. Inside was a perfect likeness of my profile, my glasses and the angle of the hat on my head. The artist seemed pleased with the $5 bill I offered in return.

The Episcopalians had the right idea about enterprise in St. Petersburg. At the entrance to their gift shop in Moscow, they handed everyone a small glass of vodka. It went easily down our thirsty throats with a very pleasant effect. I became the ideal gift shop customer. "Oh, I'll have those green drop malachite earrings and a couple of jars of that black caviar, and two of those nested dolls."

Out came the plastic and I sailed away in an afternoon vodka fog with a bag full of Russian souvenirs. Leaving,

I managed to slur out the Russian word for thank you—
spasiba.

Istanbul

In one of the thousands of tiny shops in Istanbul's teeming Grand Bazaar, I found a colorful handbag hanging from the ceiling along with hundreds of others. "How much is this?" I asked.

The shopkeeper held up another bag. "This one's cheaper. You look very sweet, but broke."

I left his shop without either bag, chuckling to myself. How did he know I really was broke? I'd spent my last euros in a Turkish bath the evening before.

The brochure for the *hamam* read: "You can catch your own inner peace with history and water in our *hamam*." Yes. We would top off our trip with a real Turkish bath. When would we ever be in Istanbul again?

A van appeared at our hotel and soon we were careening through crowded narrow streets to stop at an elaborate carved door in a dome-topped stone building. The entrance room was quiet with mahogany walls and soft exotic Middle Eastern music in the background. We sat on cushioned seats and exchanged our shoes for wooden slippers. Following the attendant to the next room, we disrobed and donned a pair of red-and-white plaid boxer shorts and a wrap of the same material for our tops.

Clacking our way through warm marble halls, we entered a spacious steamy room with a huge octagonal marble slab in the center. Directed to lie on the warm slab, like pieces of cheese left out in the sun, we gazed at brightness coming through round openings in the domed ceiling. Lying on our backs, sweat dripped from our faces into our ears, as kind of stupor overcame us for about fifteen minutes.

Suddenly, four nubile young men, called *telaks*, garbed in red-and-white plaid boxers, entered smiling and picked us up out of our puddles. They led us into two anterooms and half-threw us on bedsized marble slabs.

"You are singers," my *telak* said, then crooned.

"Whooo-haaaah."

"Whooo-haaaah," I sang back.

Turning me on my stomach, he hit me in the back of the legs with something that felt like a pillow filled with suds. After massaging my legs, he whacked me on my back again with the strange wetness and continued to massage.

Then he flipped me like a pancake and I saw he really was whacking me with a pillow filled with suds.

Then, sitting me up, "You want shampoo?"

"Mmmah," I sputtered. My hair was already wet—might as well. He filled a bowl with water from the room's marble sink, quickly flinging the contents directly at my head. I shut my eyes against the onslaught of rinsing and sudsing, and I could tell from the sounds of the others that they were getting the same treatment.

Finally, my *telak* smiled and sang a final "O - K." As the stupor lifted, we staggered again in our wooden shoes into a dressing room where we were given a dry set of red-and-white plaid wraps. Swaddled in dry towels, we sat like potentates on carpeted benches, sipping hot apple tea in a glass cup.

These exotic settings were beginning to distance me from grief and anger, rinsing off my self-pity. Gaining our equilibrium, we dressed and boarded the van to return to the hotel—broke, yes, but sweeter for the memory.

Strange Hands

"Watch out for Gypsies," the tour guide warned us. "Here in Prague they will pick your wallet out of your bag and you won't even know it. When you are out in public, be very careful with your belongings."

Each day someone in our large touring chorus had their wallet stolen. I was surrounded by nervous people who had either been victimized, or afraid they might be.

My roommate's black leather-bound personal calendar was taken.

"I'd rather have my wallet stolen," she lamented. "Now I have to reconstruct my whole life when I get back to work at the college library."

Unfazed by the warnings, I wandered around Prague by myself, a city known to rival Paris in its beauty. High above the Old Town Square, the exquisitely complicated astronomical clock ticked away, telling the time in three different formats over a calendar devoted to the signs of the zodiac. I sat for a while, watching the passing tourists, looking for Gypsies who might bump into me with the purpose of distracting my wariness as they unburdened me of my few korunas. All I knew about

Gypsies I learned from Verdi's operas, so I looked for colorfully dressed men and women who might be dancing or selling mysterious potions. But no one made eye contact, nor offered to tell my fortune.

After rehearsals for our big concert with Prague's orchestral chorus, we were free to explore the shop windows glittering with famous Czech crystal. At first, I browsed and left without buying, but the next day, I decided to go back to get a set of multifaceted candlestick holders as a wedding present for my niece.

Leaving our hotel in the rush hour before dinner, I boarded a trolley packed with riders. There were no vacant seats and barely room to stand. Clutching my purse in my left hand and frantically reaching around to grab a railing for my other one, strange hands directed my shoulders, turning me a bit while another hand took my wrist to an empty place on the railing above. Heart pounding, I held on tightly to keep my balance on the jiggling, swaying trolley ride. Certain this was my turn to be robbed and clenching my purse even more tightly to my chest, I clung where mysterious hands had placed me.

The doors opened, allowing my escape. I checked my purse. Everything was still there, wallet included. I regretted my fear that day in Prague and rather wished I had known the Czech word for "thank you."

Discoveries in Worms

One Sunday, our Presbyterian choir at home sang *Locus Iste*: *This place was made by God a peculiar mystery; it is without reproof!"* The text, written by Anton Bruckner in 1869 is a Latin prayer of dedication. I was transported back to the Old Synagogue at Worms in Germany, reconstructed after being severely damaged by the Nazis in 1938. The Davidson Singers had performed the same piece in Latin in the Cathedral in Cologne The meaning of the words, filled us with the tragedy of that place as it truly seemed truly *a deo factus est,* made by God. It was a bit overwhelming to be in a synagogue dating to 1034. Singing there, we felt the impact of the small, plain stone room which seemed to retell its story of centuries of oppression and tragedy.

Becoming close to that history enabled me to put my anxiety about the future in perspective. It helped to open me to the plight of others attached to this place who had suffered during my lifetime.

My tour roommate, Shelley Zipper, is a New York City high school English teacher whose mother had been born in Worms. She found the name of her great grandfather on a plaque in the synagogue with the names of the last members of the congregation and learned he had been sent from Worms to the Belzec concentration camp where he perished. It was good to learn that the synagogue at Worms was now also a museum devoted to the truth of what happened to its people. It has survived in spite of hatred, in spite of the regime that decimated those who worshiped God there.

I was with Shelley when she found the house where her mother was born. We didn't knock on the door because the people living there were not her family, but one of the many whose forebearers took advantage of the flight of the Jews from that place. There was a bitter taste in our mouths. That hijacked house merited much reproof, unlike the stone synagogue. Devoid of the glittering gold of other sanctuaries, it seemed truly *Locus Iste*, a place made holy.

If Jim were still with me, I wonder if I would have visited so many historic places. However, if we could have afforded the price for both of us, I believe he have tolerated everything our choral tours required. As we rehearsed after breakfast, or lunch, he would have put on his hat and sneakers and gone off to see the city, which is exactly what he did when we landed in Rome, the first and only time we traveled to Europe together.

Elderhostel

The Hualapai woman fitting us with life preservers said, "Do what the guide tells you to do." Hearing that admonition and eyeing the roiling rapids a short distance away, our excitement gave way to some trepidation. The raft accommodated a dozen rafters sitting around the edges. As the guide started the outboard engine in the back, one woman suggested we join hands and offer a prayer, which we all earnestly did.

To know about the Grand Canyon is to hope to see it. With this program, I could not only see the Grand Canyon, but also have a rafting adventure on the Colorado River. The Elderhostel program (now known as Road Scholars) was offered by the Hualapai tribe of Native Americans whose economy is largely based on tourism due to their proximity to the Grand Canyon and the Colorado River. It seemed a good choice for a widow who *is getting-on-with-her-life*.

A cousin in Phoenix drove me to northwestern part of Arizona where I picked up the Yavapai College shuttle to the lodge at Peach Spring, the tribal capital. I was told the Hualapai did not consider opening a casino because they are so close to Las Vegas. Instead, they use their location on the only road access to the Colorado to provide rafting trips. They built a new lodge to house tourists, so we weren't really roughing it.

After checking in, I hiked up the ridge in back to get my first glimpse of the canyon rim and enjoy a box lunch. The canyon was a monumental pink rift in the flat land above the rim. To view this rift was to be diminished and uplifted at the same time. We didn't want to turn from it, but it was time. I lifted my backpack from the ground to carry to the lodge for an afternoon lecture. Tiny cactus needles hitched a ride on my backpack, landing on my skin. One of the women in the group helped me get most of the stingers out, but some were left to pick out of my back for weeks afterward.

The first few days were spent in sessions learning about desert critters, tribal economics and culture. On our rafting day, we drove for an hour down a rutted road to the canyon in a sweltering old school bus. The access road washes out every time it rains, so they use giant caterpillar tractors to clear the boulders. Bumping our way to the river, we learned the rapids would be affected by the release of water from an upstream dam. The turbulence of the rapids is classified on a scale of one to ten. We hoped this day's number five classification would be perfect.

Shortly we were in the rapids. When the first wave passed, a kayaker appeared in the hollow before the next one. He slipped between the two pontoons and under the raft toward the motor. We shouted to the guide, who turned off the motor immediately, then held our breath. A few long seconds later, the kayaker spit out between the pontoons, upside down. After another anxious moment, he righted the kayak and slipped out of the way. Tragedy averted, perhaps by prayer?

Traveling down the river toward the west, we cruised alternately through a series of rollercoaster rapids that revved up our adrenalin, then calm sections where we could appreciate the towering magnificence of the cathedral-like canyon walls and marvel at the fishhook barrel cactus, 100 years old, yet only two feet wide. One mile deep in the earth, the river carved out ancient layers of rock. We could almost touch the 1.75 billion year-old Vishnu basement rock, gaining a new appreciation of the enormity of the geologic time.

Stopping at a nearby little waterfall, we scrambled to sit under its cool tumble as a relief from the 102-degree heat in the canyon's depth before enjoying a riparian lunch brought by the guides. By contrast, back in the raft, we were constantly hit hard in the face and chest by waves of 52-degree river water. Six wet hours later, the river widened and calmed. Coming around the last curve, the shore opened enough to accommodate a couple of waiting helicopters. Like dragonflies dipping in for a drink, they were ferrying well-dressed sightseers flown in from Los Vegas. They stood under a ramada, enjoying champagne from fluted plastic glasses.

Sans champagne, and damp all over, we lined up to tell our honest weight to a woman seated at a table in the shade. After that painful revelation, they equalized our mass and divided us into groups of four or five for the flight back to the top of the canyon.

I was seated behind the pilot next to the door of the glass bubble with almost a 360-degree view above and below. On the way up, I realized I had no problem with heights; I did have a problem with depths. Unable to see the bottom, but ascending close beside the vertical canyon wall, it seemed if I tightened every muscle in my body and curled my toes tightly while making little "yip-yip" sounds, the chopper could go straight up over the rim and land at the nearest airport. There, the old yellow school bus waited to drive us through cactus-lined Joshua Tree National Park road for a few hours, returning us to the lodge and a hot shower to shuck off accumulations of red river dirt. Since then, the Hualapai have constructed a skywalk that juts over the rim for what must be a wondrous unique experience.

I am certain Jim would have preferred to stay on solid ground because I once convinced him to get in my little sailboat. As soon as we had the sail up and moved away from the dock, he insisted I take him right back and got out of the boat. Clearly, he could not tolerate being under control of the wind as well as his wife. I knew that Jim, with his habit of ranking experiences on a one to ten, and his dislike of riding in unpredictable watery vessels, would have ranked this a two, maybe a one.

For me, this had been more than a check off the bucket list. It satisfied my need for adventure and showed me more possibilities of how to manage on my own. Although many times I wished Jim were with me, my single-life choices would not have been his and I continued to seek out more travel opportunities. One of the best was to spend a week at Chautauqua Institute. I signed up for a course in personal essay writing and a short course in soaring.

Soaring

"You have the controls. You're flying." I hadn't expected to learn how to fly a glider, nor to learn very much about soaring. However, I leapt at the chance to fly in a sailplane when I saw it listed in the brochure. It would be a great way to top off my two-week stay at Chautauqua Institute in western New York State, a demonstration in the sky—a lark literally and figuratively.

I watched as the other gliders took off into the perfect weather. Weighing 500-600 pounds loaded, the two-seat sailplanes were built like a graceful, giant white bird, with a wingspan of 40 feet. Small planes must reach a speed of 65 mph before they can lift off; the lighter sailplanes are airborne seconds sooner, impatient to sail aloft into the puffy cumulous clouds and disappear into the light. Counting the amount of time it took for a motorized Piper Cub to tow us up to 2,500 feet, the whole experience was supposed to take 20 minutes.

When it was my turn, Ian, the FAA-certified commercial pilot, sat behind me with his own controls and began my instruction in the sky. First, I learned gliders are powered by the energy in the heat thermals rising from the earth on a sunny day. Because lakes absorb the sun's heat, we avoided flying directly over them. Instead, we spiraled between Lake Chautauqua and Lake Erie, circling round and round, riding the thermal energy coming from farmers' fields and open meadows.

At one point, we rose at 600 feet per minute, but also descended at the same rate before we could find another thermal of rising air. The otherworldly sensation was neither rising up nor sinking; we seemed to float under the clouds. Ian explained that the cumulous clouds were darkest because they were filled with moisture from stronger thermals providing the best lift. He drew my attention to the instruments on the cockpit in front of me.

"Look at the altimeter. Now we are at 3,000 feet, 500 feet higher than when the plane released us." I could now see far on to Lake Erie. He directed my gaze to the horizon. "On clear days, we can see Canada at this height and there's the Erie Peninsula in Pennsylvania."

As we spiraled around to see how high we could go, I felt the strength of the sun's ultraviolet rays and wished I'd worn long sleeves. The skin on my arms was burning, but I was glad to be wearing a hat and sunglasses as the Chautauqua catalog listing advised.

"I'm not using tight turns because I don't want to make you dizzy," Ian said.

"I don't mind a bit. I'm used to small planes," I replied. "Go ahead, I'll love it." He tightened the upward spiral, dropping the wing on the left, "Whoooo! This is great," I shrieked as if I was on a carnival ride.

Ian must have been favorably impressed with my reaction because when we straightened out, he urged me to put my hand on the control handle between my knees. Then he coached me to relax my arm while getting a feel for the miniscule movements needed as he worked his own controls.

"Pull up," he said.

When I pulled too far, the sailplane nose rose abruptly upwards.

"Pull down!" The nose went down in vigorous response. It takes a delicate touch to keep a glider level.

"Keep the same distance between the top of the control panel and the horizon," he instructed. Using tiny movements, I maneuvered the control handle for several intense minutes before giving it back to Ian and taking a deep breath.

After 20 minutes, with my video camera rolling, we descended quickly to land. A soft bump and a short skid brought us back to earth. Jim would not have taken the ride, but I'm certain he would have been there to send me off and smile as I returned from the sky. For me, to abandon the earth for the sky on a sunny day, soaring between Lake Erie and Chautauqua Lake that sunny day was like the freedom I used to feel powered by the wind in my little sailboat. Sailing with the wind on the water or the air left no space for grief.

Yoga Weekend

Everyone has a backache story. Mine was caused by a cockroach. While living in our small Pelham Manor apartment with our two babies, we were plagued with what the super called "water bugs." Our neighbor did some research and found they were large American cockroaches; some were at least the size of a Brazil nut. I was feeding newborn Christopher on the couch when I spied one of them traversing the fireplace mantel, headed for the kitchen. Wisely laying the baby down, I went after the thing with Raid. Undaunted, it lumbered onto my postage stamp kitchen floor. I aimed and shot thoroughly, soaking the bug and the floor. The little antediluvian monster turned and started back in my direction. Startled, I slipped backward and landed on my tailbone. Now in pain, I no longer cared where the bug had crawled.

After the initial jolt, I thought I was okay until six months later when we moved to a duplex with a backyard and clothesline. After bending down to pick up wet sheets, I couldn't straighten up again. A year later I was still going to an excellent chiropractor who treated my sore spots with pressure from his middle finger. That finger, due to injury, was just a big stump protruding from his knuckle. I also found a yoga class where I learned back-strengthening exercises.

When we moved to the Adirondacks, the local chiropractor had all his fingers, but couldn't crack my neck well. I realized then I'd have to practice yoga exercises the rest of my life to keep my back strong. It's easy to slough off when my back is feeling fine, but if I don't practice yoga postures daily, the soreness returns.

To expand my yoga practice, I spent a few weekends at Kripalu Center for Yoga and Health in the Berkshires. Built by the Jesuits, the place is on a hill overlooking picturesque Lake Mahkeenac, also known as the Stockbridge Bowl. I registered for a dormitory bed, one of 30 bunks in a room with a fantastic floor-to-ceiling view of the mountain verdure and the lake. Wall to wall windows overlooked the valley. The sun rose over the hill on the left and set behind the hill on the right, reminding me of the old Kate Smith song, "When the moon comes over the mountain, someone waits for me." The yoga center seemed like a perfect place to treat my back and at the same time deal with the stress of widowhood.

I opted for a reflexology foot massage purported to benefit one's genitals, but my back was the priority. In addition, the foot massage was meant to restore balance in my body and as they put it, "increase the flow of *chi*."

At the end of one of the sessions, we were directed to hold the final pose as long as possible. I was doing very well as the pressure to let it go mounted. Still I held, curious to see if I could withstand as long as the others, which I did. Suddenly I was overcome with sobs wracking my body. In a vain attempt to stop, I curled up in a ball on the floor, but the effort seemed to add to my reaction. Those around seemed to allow my crying jag to dissipate on its own. Maybe my days of grieving were not all behind me.

I had the same reaction a few years earlier in one other yoga session. All the sessions customarily end with the corpse pose, but in that particular day, lying there on my back, silent and still, I was overcome with the image of Jim's corpse after the coroner left him. Tears rolled down my face. The startled yoga teacher seemed to need some reason for my reaction to the pose. Explaining my vision helped calm me down. I haven't broken down as drastically in any subsequent yoga practice, but I avoid stamina poses, opting to standing on one foot and then the other as long as possible without losing my balance.

Meals at Kripalu were another adventure. When I asked directions to the cafeteria, a staffer reprimanded me: "The *dining chapel is* on the third floor." They do eat in a former chapel, and it's clearly larger than many churches. The food is mostly vegetarian, with a great array of granola, fruit and yogurt for breakfast. It's the mindful eating that was hard to do. Mindful eating, I learned, is a Zen practice of being super-aware of what you are chewing. No talking is allowed during breakfast.

In the great silence, I slid into a chair at a long table opposite two women who were quite mindful of their granola. I tried chewing a few mouthfuls, but became uneasy. It was strangely unnerving to eat while watching each other chew our granola. After a few minutes, I picked up my tray and found a table facing the wall where I could eat in private without watching others' mindful masticating.

My second yoga weekend was in winter. I looked forward to the glorious view from the dormitory room and grabbed the bottom bunk I had occupied before. It was exactly the same room except for a new wall-to-wall carpeting. Alas, I forgot to use my allergy nose spray before falling asleep. (New carpets in enclosed rooms irritate my allergies.) I woke to a gentle shake on my shoulder. "Turn over," said a voice in the dark. "You're snoring." Sleepily embarrassed, I crawled around in my bag, administered the nose spray, and went back to sleep. My slumber was interrupted a second time with the same shoulder shake and a more exasperated "*Please*, you're snoring and we can't sleep."

In the morning, right after the dawn yoga session, I slunk down to the registration desk. Shamefully I admitted what happened. The sympathetic clerk looked at my record in his computer.

"But you were here before and you didn't snore. We don't want to list you as a snorer."

"Well I don't want to be, but I guess you'll have to move me tonight."

My new single cell had only a forest view. Instead of finding nirvana, I came away in humiliation, officially a snorer.

Carnival Cruise

Alone, but in a tour group on New Year's Day 2002, I boarded a Carnival cruise ship for Pacific ports. Starting from Los Angeles that evening, the first port in the morning would be Catalina Island.

After a late dinner, we settled in our windowless cabin for the night. I fell asleep listening to the thrumming of the ship's engine. Something woke me in the middle of the night. A sensation of being on a turntable, an awareness we were changing direction woke me in the night, but putting that strange feeling aside, I returned to sleep.

The turning sensation was gone when I woke and the engine was quiet. In the morning haze on the upper deck, we could see Catalina Island, only a boat ride away. At breakfast, we struck up a conversation with a woman whose husband worked on the ship. She told us what had happened while we were sleeping.

A young man had been stricken with a drug overdose, so the captain called the Catalina Island authorities to send a helicopter to bring him to the island's hospital. But they refused because the fog was too thick to fly safely.

The captain turned the ship around and headed back to fogless Los Angeles where an emergency helicopter was waiting to assist the patient. As soon as the man was dispatched to the hospital, the ship sailed back again toward Catalina, which explained the turning sensation I felt during the night.

We heard that the man died shortly afterward from the overdose. It's comforting for a traveling widow to know that if you happen to be gravely ill, they'll turn a huge Carnival ship around, and make the effort to keep you alive.

It Happened in Maui

Armed with rented flippers and goggles, I set out to find a good place to snorkel along a mile-long stretch of sandy beach. It was another perfect day on Maui, and this was the first chance during my week's stay at a conference to find a coral patch occupied by bright fish. My colleague, Kjrsten Keane, had already departed for home, and I was now alone and determined to tend to my seldom-enjoyed passion for snorkeling that let me escape from the pressures of work and travel. Later, Kjrsten sent me an appropriate bumper sticker declaring, "I'd rather be snorkeling." She knows me well.

I was determined to find the reef world I first discovered while recovering from my short unhappy first marriage. I was in the Virgin Islands and the aptly named Sapphire Beach. There I learned to spit inside the goggles to keep the glass clear and lean into the shallow water. The glasses stayed water-tight as I found a new world.

Like a gigantic kaleidoscope, the dazzling denizens of the reef were enchanting. Pink stripes on blue, blue patches on fuchsia, jail stripes on orange, speckled, mottled, diaphanous, garish and golden. The fish all found deliberate routes, while avoiding each other between the sharp edges of the coral. Remembering to keep clear of the black spiny sea urchins that deliver a painful sting, I hovered a few feet above the coral. To swim in clear waters above the stings of life could be a metaphor for my life ever since.

Each opportunity to snorkel in Caribbean waters has been equally superb. Over the years, I found excellent snorkeling opportunities in the Yucatan, where sinkholes called cenotes are created by collapsing limestone caves. Those cenotes are filled with pure, clear water replete with amazing tropical fish. Once, with Jim at Xel-Ha near Tulum, a huge grouper floated silently by, oblivious to our alien presence. Now I was hoping to find something equally as exciting in Hawaii.

Walking along the beach, I searched the shallow water for dark patches signaling reef life, finding none. The warm sun became increasingly uncomfortable and the gear got heavier with each step along the water's edge. Impatient to be in the water, I stood on the line left by the last wave and set both flippers on the sand in front of my feet. Just as I put a flipper on one foot and one toe in the other, a wave rolled up, grabbed the flipper from my toe, and took it away into the surf near three women who were standing together in the water talking.

"Hey! The wave took my flipper in the water. Do you see it there?"

All three looked around and shook their heads. With one flipper missing, I realized I would have to pay full price to replace the pair. Nevertheless, I was determined to save what I could from the rental. Waddling into the surf, I found I could swim fairly well with one flipper. Using gentle kicks, it was easy to maintain my position in the vacillating drift, becoming another occupant of the sea. I had been swimming along the shoreline for a few minutes in my search for something to see besides a sandy bottom when a huge sea turtle glided by. I tried to keep up with the turtle, but it was too fast, so I stood up and looked around.

One of the ladies who had been standing where I lost the flipper was following me, brandishing it. Amid watery and effusive thanks, I realized this woman had been trying to return the flipper to me for some time. In order to put the lost flipper on my other foot, I had to crawl out of the shallow surf, which wanted to keep me in the water as it had the flipper. Making it to the last few inches of depth, but still buffeted by the wave action, I struggled to haul myself out. Like the first prehistoric fish coming onto land, I was crawling on my hands and knees, struggling against the push and pull, when two able-bodied men appeared and lifted me out by both arms.

Suddenly, finding the reef and its fish was no longer my heart's desire. Seeing the turtle would suffice. It was time to learn my limitations and appreciate that I was returning with all my rented gear intact thanks to helpful strangers that day on the Hawaiian island of Maui.

Chapter V

Getting by With a Little Help From My Friends

All our loneliness and worry and fear seem to fade in the presence of a friend who never judges, but stands alongside with loyalty.

Joyce Sequichie Hifler

Blaming God

Prayer is not my normal mode. This was not always so. My well-meaning mother had long ago doused my inclination to prayer. When I was a devout 12-yearold, she found me in my bedroom, talking aloud to God.

I still remember the tension in her voice. "I know you think you talk to God..."

I didn't hear what followed, too overcome with shame and embarrassment to listen, picking up some of her fear that her daughter might have the mental illness in her husband's side of the family. That fear mortified my young soul and made me wary of ever praying again, out loud, or silently.

Prayer appears to work for the devout. Entering into a prayerful state seems to give them comfort as they summon the attention of the Almighty. It's too hard to wrap my mind around that possibility, but for those who ignore the laws of physical science, it seems to work.

Not long after Jim died, still smarting with grief, and perhaps, blaming God, I sought help from friends Al and Alice Macnab. Al had become a deacon in the Episcopal faith, and I thought they could answer my questions. At a time when I should have become more spiritual, I was a doubting Thomas.

"We say 'Thank God' whenever good things happen. If God has a hand in everything that happens, why can't we blame him for the bad things as well?" I asked.

They answered, "Read the Book of Job. Many bad things happened to him, but he never gave up believing in God."

"So God takes the credit, but not the blame."

"There is no answer," they told me, "God is good, and we are human, subject to all the inadequacies of humanity."

"I suppose that includes death," I concluded.

Best Friend

One night when it was my turn to stay home with the boys, Jim returned from choir rehearsal, excited about the new soprano who had joined the church with her husband. "What a great voice. And a very attractive woman too."

I was jealous until I met Bobbi Damp, and over the years we would become best friends. I was her biggest fan. Jim was right about her voice. I'd rather listen to Bobbi Damp sing than anyone. I cherish the times we sang together, especially the recording of our duet from Vivaldi's *Gloria*. On that recording, it was hard to tell our voices apart because we rehearsed together so much. A part of me was lost when she died of lung cancer on Labor Day in 2015. The loss inspired me to write this eulogy, patterned after the one Al Macnab wrote for Jim's memorial service:

Dear Rev. Simon Peter,

Please accept this letter of recommendation and reference for Ms. Barbara Blake Damp who has left us to enter your heavenly community.

I have known "Bobbi" since we first met at church where we both sang in the choir. You will want her gorgeous voice in the heavenly choir where her high notes are as lovely as any heard on heaven or earth. Also, she could be used to direct senior adult choirs, preparing them to sing despite any of their physical limitations. Her brilliant smile and musical knowledge would charm the angels, whether rehearsing a bell choir or voices of some of your elder angels.

Wherever you have an opening for teacher, you will find Bobbi can apply her experience as a first-grade teacher or high school choir director with joyful creativity. She had her own dance studio, where preschool cherubs learned tap and ballet. (I hope you like the idea of cherubs wearing tap shoes). She was a great musical song and dance choreographer for divine community productions of "The Music Man."

"Brigadoon," "Oklahoma" or an original "Disney on Parade" production that she

arranged. She was an unforgettable Golda in "The Fiddler on the Roof," so don't forget to include her in those auditions.

You may already have witnessed her retirement community musical adaption of "The Wizard of Oz," that showcased her men's and women's choirs. However, if some seniors want to learn how to tap dance or enjoy evenings of line dancing, she's the one to use. By the way, once you place Bobbi in a band as the drummer, everyone will start tapping their feet because playing drums is another of her many talents.

You might also consider Bobbi's skills as an event organizer. If you want to advertise a Christmas production or May Day parade, she's your gal. If asked, she'll not only produce and promote the event, she'll be the best soprano in the chorus.

For many summers, she was the Executive Director of the Adirondack Festival of American Music in Saranac Lake where she attended to every detail, including hauling orchestra chairs and directing the proper placement of choir risers.

With her as my right-hand helper on fundraising for the AFAM Scholarship Committee, we began the first Messiah Sing-in. I'm told the community still gets together to sing this wonderful Handel piece on the first weekend of December.

Bobbi's husband has been waiting for her to join him since he died in 2013. As you already know, Bob and Bobbi moved around many times for his insurance and real estate business, making huge contributions to each community's church life. You can expect Bobbi will be one of your Celestial Rotary members, continuing on as one of the first women to join that club. When Bobbi was crowned Queen of the Saranac Lake Winter Carnival, she choreographed the Rotary events.

I would consider nominating her for sainthood. Here's why. As soon as Bob could retire, they sold their lake house and moved to Kentucky where they could join her sister Ann in caring for their aging mother. But the main reason she should be canonized is because when she was in the early stages of cancer, she continued working in the long-term care section of their retirement community, spending hours feeding and assisting the nurses. Few saints could say they did that. If she can't be officially canonized because Protestants don't have them, but surely there is a wonderful mansion up there for this couple.

With all the demands on her time, Bobbi and I continued to develop our friendship embroidered with great belly laughs. In fact, if you have any grieving widows who feel unappreciated, she could not only accept their mood, she would actually improve it. When I wanted to feel better about anything, I knew I could call her and the hurt would dissipate. Sometimes in our friendship there were moments when, like a child learning to walk, I needed someone to take my hand until I could stand on my own. Every widow should be so blessed. Every widow can make it through with a friend like Bobbi.

I know from personal experience that she can make the best chicken soup to cure a cold, teach a beginner how to use a computer and, if she finds you in the winter with cold toes exposed by a cast, she can whip up a toe cozy from a furry scrap in a few minutes.

Lastly, if all those jobs are filled, she also has credentials as a writer, poet and editor. I am dedicating my memoir to her for all her editing and the story organization guidance she applied to it.

Let me assure you that this is a good woman, jolly fun and quite responsible. I hope you won't mind her custom of pouring a tall gin and tonic with lime at 4 p.m. each afternoon. There has to be something to slow her down enough to sleep through the night.

Bobbi Damp probably doesn't need my recommendation, but she brings the love and admiration of her friends and family with her. She's been our wonder woman, and we miss her very much. Now she is yours.

Sincerely,
Miriam S. Russell

Thank You for the Music

As a teenager assigned to clean my room, I would spend winter Saturday afternoons halfheartedly cleaning while listening to the Texaco broadcasts from the Metropolitan Opera. In 1963, when Jim brought me to my first live opera in, a performance of "Adriana Lecouvreur" with Renata Tebaldi and Franco Corelli, the big stars of the '60s, it was the realization of my fondest wish. Tall, dark Corelli appeared onstage all in black, wearing a pair of thigh-high black leather boots. As he threw off his voluminous white satin-lined cape and embraced the soprano, I nearly fell out of the balcony. His entrance would have been enough, but then he sang in an easy, soaring glorious tenor. Jim used to say he didn't have to do anything in the way of foreplay afterward. I was already turned on!

There was a time shortly after Jim died when a few chords of "Che gelida manina" from "La Boheme," would put me in the throes of sobs because it had been his favorite. While driving with my friend Joan Tyler shortly after Jim died, I made the mistake of playing a tape of Cilea's "Adriana Lecouvreur" in the car, my tears started to flow, and I had to pull over to the side of the road to avoid an accident. When Joan returned to home and learned Bobbi was coming to visit me, she warned, "Don't let her play any opera tapes while driving." At any rate, breaking down unexpectedly was a bit too scary and I vowed then not to listen to opera again.

Not knowing about my recent avowal when I visited Bob and Bobbi in Louisville, they treated me with tickets to the Opera to see "Turandot." Remembering the performance Jim and I saw with Corelli and Neilson, I was afraid of becoming too emotional. Fortunately, I kept my trepidations to myself and discovered I could appreciate the performance quite well without breaking down. Thanks to my friends, I was able to pick up Jim's musical legacy to admire anew.

I regret Jim can't see the visual advancements in Metropolitan Opera performances. Using a recent Cirque du Soleil-inspired staging of Berlioz's "Damnation of Faust," choristers appeared suddenly out of the darkness while angels flew above them and Marguerite walked vertically up a ladder to heaven.

The love scene in "Romeo and Juliet" was also unforgettable. The curtain opened on the lovers on a bed suspended midair. A strong breeze caused the bed sheets to sway, while Roberto Alagna and Anna Netrebko appeared to be naked, arms and legs twisting around each other, singing their hearts out about what a shame Romeo has to leave Juliet on their wedding night.

Fortunately, I have a small circle of friends who enjoy a full schedule of concertizing and opera going: Paul Trela, Elizabeth Bergen, Roberta Farrell, Steve Carmel and sometimes my sister and brother with spouses Karim and Carol. We treat ourselves to performances full of unexpected surprises and imagination.

On the other hand, not all our forays into summer opera performances are joyful. In fact, Mascagni's *Iris,* performed at the Bard College in the summer of 2016 was not only ugly and nasty, it was misogynistic and repulsive with little to redeem it. After the second act, we were bent on leaving, but decided to see if the third act would pull the plot out from the constant mistreatment of a virginal woman from a sexual predator into some kind of punishment for him and relief for Iris' torture.

Regretfully, the plot actually slid into the sewer where she dies under her last glimpse of the sun amidst the trash. The critic, James Jordan, astutely writing in "The Observer" noted, *'Iris'* Might Be The Most Fucked Up Opera Ever."

One other of Mascagni's operas performed often is Cavalleria Rusticana; his "Intermezzo" is one of the loveliest pieces ever written. It would have been a much better expenditure of time and money than to dig poor Iris up after 100 years. Sometimes, if a piece hasn't been performed for that long, there is a good reason.

A Carol in Autumn

"Jean died this morning."

Bob Martin was on the phone, telling me that on this lovely October day, his wife Jean had lost her long painful fight with cancer. As a couple, they had been a wonderful support to me after Jim died. I remembered they were the first at my door that fateful day.

Jean Martin started her doctoral program while working full time as the reading consultant with an office opposite mine in the school. She inspired me to pursue a doctoral program myself. We shared problems, solutions and triumphs together as we worked toward our common goal which she achieved a year before I did.

I always knew I was welcome to spend the night at their home or their place at the beach in Delaware any time I was on my way north to be with family or returning south to the Eastern Shore. Once, after attending Bobbi's daughter Katie and David Klossner's New Year's Eve wedding in the Adirondacks, I stopped at their place in Delaware with a bottle of wine that had frozen solid in my car trunk overnight and exploded on the trip south while defrosting. As a result, my car smelled like a bar. Shortly after I arrived, Bob removed the broken glass, took out the spare tire, and sopped up the pooled red liquid. Jean and I were laughing at the thought of what might have happened if I had been stopped for a traffic violation with that unmistakable smell wafting from my car.

Jean and Bob seemed to show up like a *deus ex machina* whenever I needed urgent help. They suddenly appeared and organized a fireman's carry to get me from my position flat on my back beside the Country Club pool as I lay writhing after popping my Achilles tendon. Strangers all around averted their eyes to my distress, but Jean commandeered the help of a muscular swimmer and between the three of them, I was dispatched to the hospital.

Bob asked, "Would you sing at her funeral?"

"You bet," I answered. "Perhaps a rendition of 'On Eagle's Wings' from Psalm 91 would be good?"

"Well, Jean loved Christmas carols. Would you sing a carol?"

Putting down the phone, I picked up a book of carols, and opened it. "Joy to the World" shone from the page. I knew all the verses by heart.

At the funeral home, the minister was arranging the ceremony and Bob explained I was going to sing.

"What are you singing?"

"Joy to the World," I ventured.

I watched his face wince a bit above his clerical collar.

"I've never had a Christmas carol sung at a funeral before." he said.

"Jean liked Christmas carols," I insisted, "though I had never sung one at a funeral before." With my own reservations, I was standing behind Bob's choice. The bereaved should have their way.

The room in the funeral home was long and narrow. I stood next to the coffin, no microphone or piano to support me. Curious faces gazed up as I explained I was singing a Christmas carol at the request of the deceased. I took a deep breath and found a note in a comfortable key:

Joy to the world, the Lord is come;
Let earth receive her king.
Let every heart prepare him room
And Heaven and nature sing,
And Heaven and nature sing.

I saw some small smiles appear on faces as I gathered strength for the next verse. With a huge breath, I held up the sound:

The glories of his righteousness
And wonders of his love
And wonders of his love.

Earth, heaven, joy, receive, love: Somehow the words conveyed a meaningful message in this setting. The glory and the promise of Christmas seemed to relieve the sorrow of death. I think Jean would have liked it. Mother, Dad and Jim, all my lost ones, might have liked it as well.

Life and Death

Until she was 22 years old, our cat Sadie managed to jump up on the mantle, endangering a few pieces of Mother's hand-painted china. Jim once observed that cats keep going strong right up until the end. Sadie was like that until after work one day I found her under the piano bench, curled up in the same position as I left her. I took her to the vet. Years before, when our Welsh terrier, Cookie, was euthanized, Jim and Matt took her to the vet. Now I had to see it was done for Sadie, a very old cat at 22.

It tore at my core to stand by her on the table, feeling life leave her. I'd never been at the actual moment of death before—the instant of the end—the great divide between life and death. Was this how it had been for Jim? An instant of great pain, then nothingness? Or is there a perception of a tunnel with light at the end—a sense of traveling through—a leave taking? Nevertheless, the moment, even with Sadie's little life, made me dizzy with the loss—another loss.

Perhaps those who miss being present when their loved ones die should not regret it. What if Jim had been in my arms? I think it might have damaged me more than finding him on the floor, already gone from life.

You had come back from a walk—down to the harbor-carrying the old shillelagh you used to ward away menacing dogs. The neighbors told me they saw you that day, shortly before I found you. Was it lucky you didn't die slowly—aging bit by bit like most of us left here?

Three deaths in three years, first Dad, then Jim, now Sadie, the third loss—this burial witnessed only by me and my neighbor. I hoped that according to the superstition bad things happen in threes, my complement of tragedies was full.

Licking my wounds, I focused on my doctoral projects and papers. Learning became my life. After each day at work, I would devour articles and texts. Issues and theories, technology and educational issues took the emptiness out of coming home to a silent house.

The following fall, I was notified that my final applied dissertation and coursework were complete and was awarded a Doctorate in Education. Full of the satisfaction one feels at the attainment of a long-sought goal, I purchased the doctoral degree regalia and wore it for the graduation ceremony in Florida. I sent my picture, grinning ear-to- ear and gripping my diploma, to mother who was then in the nursing home. She had been suffering from frequent strokes. Matt told me she kept her fingertips on the picture for a long time, smiling broadly, unable to speak.

Armed with my credentials, I would set off to give the world of education the benefit of my wealth of knowledge. I would make a difference. Perhaps I should have known getting the degree was the easy part; finding the proper place to use it was much harder.

Widow with a Doctorate

I thought I wanted to live near Virginia Davidson and my new friends in New York so I could be a year-round Davidson Singer, able walk the streets of the city daily. One day on a corner near Times Square on 42nd Street, a woman stopped me and asked, "Excuse me, do you speak English?" She wanted to find clothing shops. I laughed and directed her to Madison Avenue. I would start a new life among it all.

My toe-hold, after leaving the Eastern Shore, was Virginia's cozy two-room apartment on West 89th Street. One room was lined with file cabinets filled with choral music and the grand piano in the center. The other room was a bed-sitter where her voice students waited their turn. The window side was her office, her bed and the TV. A door led to a small balcony loaded with plants in the summer. Staying there sometimes when she was away, it became a place for much needed certainty, where I could feel a sense of belonging. Virginia had offered to keep some little things temporarily that I couldn't bear to live with after Jim died: his little bust of Puccini and his framed old Met stamps, the Puccini CDs I couldn't listen to until years later; a picture of the old Met curtain and the small curtain square he purchased when the old Met was demolished. All had a temporary perch on the top of her bookshelf, reminding me of him.

One year during the Christmas holidays when Virginia was in her Florida home, I stayed on 89th Street for a few days, hunkering down under her comforters, among her pillows, escaping for a while before gathering my courage again to set off in search of my new life.

In November 1998, five years into widowhood, and armed with a doctorate in education, I was hardly ready for retirement. I spent over 30 years as a public school speech therapist, a job I had loved, but now I wanted a new challenge—an encore career.

Not in the System

One New York Times ad urged teachers to apply in New York City public schools and earn a good salary. It seemed like a possibility. In spite of wanting to do something different, I applied and was interviewed by Harriet in the Special Education Office. There was an opening for a speech therapist in an elementary school in the Bronx because one of the therapists was leaving. The school was in the middle of one of the most impoverished areas of the borough. I wanted to visit before making a decision, so I asked to spend a day with the speech therapist whose position I would take. A visit was arranged for the next day.

At 9:30 a.m., school was already in session at the prewar five-story brick building with a tiny playground nearby. The front door opened on a landing with steel stairways, and the uniformed guard directed me to the office on the second floor. The principal's door was closed; he wasn't in sight.

I approached a secretary at one of the desks.

"Your name?"

"Miriam Russell."

"I don't have your name here."

"I'm from the district Special Education Office to meet with the speech therapist who's leaving. But first I need to speak to the building special education supervisor."

The payroll supervisor, overhearing our conversation, called me over to her desk. "Do you have a license?"

"I have New York State certification. I've applied for a New York City license. Here are some papers signed by the district speech supervisor."

"Do you have a file number?"

"Yes, it's on this paper," I said, producing the paper. "When I was at Court Street yesterday, they agreed to expedite the fingerprinting I did two weeks ago."

She called the Board of Education and gave them my number then put the phone down. "You're not in the system," she informed me.

"I'm shadowing the person presently in the position today to see the children and the school."

"You can't do that. You're not in the system yet. You don't have a license. When were you going to start?"

"On the 30th."

"Well you can't start until you're in the system and have a New York City license."

"I don't want to work today, just observe."

"You can't do that. The district people don't understand. We can't let anyone in who isn't in the system and you're not in the system."

"Try calling Harriet, the district supervisor," I suggested.

She repeated her admonitions to Harriet, "The regulations don't allow anyone to be hired without a New York City license."

"Could I speak to Harriet?"

She handed the phone to me.

Harriet explained, "They don't understand we are trying to fill the position because the speech therapist is leaving. Ask them to page the special education supervisor. She'll take you to meet the therapist."

It was almost 10:30 when the special education supervisor appeared. I introduced myself and explained my mission.

"Cheryl isn't here today, but I'll introduce you to Candy, who is the other speech therapist," she said matter of factly.

I followed her up to the third floor, watching her sneakered shoes ascend the grimy, steep stairs, thinking, *boy, I would develop thighs of steel traveling these stairs every day.*

"This is the special education floor," she announced. A boy ran by us in the hall, yelling. She tried to grab him, but he pulled away, smashing into the glass door of a display case, shattering it over the floor.

"Get in there!" she yelled as she pushed him into a room. "Get in my office and sit down!" The boy ran around in the office.

"Sit down and be quiet!" He continued running around, yelling back at her until she got him out into another room. Children ran in and out. She yelled at each one of them about something; apparently, the special education building supervisor's job involved discipline by vocal volume. It didn't look very effective. Was this a typical day in her office?

She led me to Candy's office, down a narrow hall and up a flight of stairs. Candy was about to leave to prepare for a baby shower for one of the staff members.

"OK, if you can't meet with me now, let's have lunch," I suggested since it was nearly noon.

"Oh no, I have to meet with the party committee."

"When will you be back?"

"Around one."

"I'll meet you here at one o'clock. Meanwhile, could you show me the office I would be using?"

Up another short set of stairs, Candy unlocked the door at the top. It must have been a storage room since there was barely space for a teacher's desk and one student's desk, but little else. The single dirty window was boarded up from outside.

"Could I see some student files?"

"I don't know where they are. I have to go now."

We returned to the supervisor's office. I was hoping to talk to her, but she suggested I talk with the teacher next door. After telling her students to sit down and be quiet, this teacher told me about the difficulties of teaching here. She confessed she really didn't like the job. She kept reminding her students to sit down and wait for lunch. This school seemed to be all about the teachers. There were baby showers to plan and it was okay to take time to complain to a prospective teacher like me. The most important factor seemed to be to get in the "system" of special licenses. I was getting impatient. It was noon and I decided to get some lunch.

I questioned the guard at the front door landing.

"When I start next week and park in the parking lot, can I get inside the building through the side door at 8 a.m.?"

"I don't have any control over that door. Come in the front door."

"Who has control over the side door?"

"The custodian, but technically the staff isn't supposed to be here until 8:40."

I wondered why the teachers weren't allowed in the building until 20 minutes before the children.

I walked through the empty playground and bought a sandwich at a delicatessen across the street. Returning to the playground, I wondered why none of the 634 children in the school were playing there. I found a bench and sat to eat my sandwich, reassuring myself that this Bronx neighborhood was perfectly fine. But where were the children and teacher aides? I was impatient to get back to speak with the other therapist. She would be my partner, a key person to help me learn my way around.

At 1 p.m., I found Candy's locked office door and knocked. She wasn't back yet. I waited until 1:30. Apparently, Candy was too busy with her shower plans. The children on her schedule wouldn't see her today. Nor would the children who were supposed to get help from the absent therapist I was to replace.

As I started back toward Ms. W's noisy office, I wondered how much time that therapist actually spent with the children who needed her help. I realized this situation wasn't for me. I couldn't be a part of a place full of staff that put children last. I walked down the stairs and out of the building.

About a year later, I received an official license to teach in New York City public schools in my mailbox. I had given up the idea living in New York City and bought a townhouse upstate. Now I was officially in the system, but had already moved on.

This had to be the toughest part. Surely life would open up some real possibilities after this. I had to find a better fit for myself; perhaps I had been looking in the wrong places.

More Hurdles

One of the rules widows are supposed to obey is a negative: Don't make major life changes in the first year. Don't sell the house and move to Florida. Deal with the pain in familiar surroundings. I stayed in my house in Virginia, obeying those rules for six years, but it was time to go home to be near my son and dying mother. I often had to take emergency flights home as Mother's hospitalizations and her fast-acting dementia became more serious; each time we thought she might be dying.

Matt was already with his grandmother because he was new to the area and needed a place to live while starting a new job. Fortunately, he was there to call for an ambulance when she had an attack in the night that led to a period of hospitalization and the nursing home for the rest of her life. When she arrived there, she stood in the lunchroom, looked around and proclaimed, "You're all in here to die," whereupon, she sat down and never put a complete sentence together again.

For all the previous years, I lived hours away, leaving my sister and her husband to attend to my mother's needs. They would call my brother, who lived a bit further away, to assist. Although I had a good job and wonderful friends on the Eastern Shore, it was time to move back and share some of the burden. After deciding to quit my job on the Eastern shore, I called my sister to tell her my plans, thinking she'd be glad.

She wasn't, and neither was my brother. The extent of their opposition to my coming home and temporarily moving into Mother's home astounded me. My sister explained that they always had the responsibility of Mother and Dad and it had been very hard for them, but still, I was quite hurt. My confusion gave way to stress; I was feeling a sort of victimhood.

I admit I had not been much help over the years; I deliberately avoided getting involved in our parents' issues. My relationship with Mother, while never without problems, became a detriment to her health. Once at her home, I drove her to a doctor's appointment for a minor procedure. Along the 20-mile trip, she became increasingly agitated about my driving. "You drive just like your father," she reminded me, as I recalled her low opinion of his accident-free driving habits. The doctor sent her home without the procedure because her blood pressure was too high. My help was a hindrance at that point.

In spite of everything, I returned to live in her house with Matt. It seemed ideal for me to join him there to pay all the taxes and house expenses during mother's hospitalizations. As her condition deteriorated and costs of her medical care mounted, we sold her house. Still waiting to sell my own house in Virginia, I moved into an apartment near her nursing home while I continued my job search and my musical tours.

In the face of all the stress, it helped a bit to remember a motto I found on a three by five card in Jim's desk—the desk that bruised him as he fell to the floor the moment he slipped instantly from living: *If it's not fatal, it's not important.*

Toughing It Out

Finding that encore job, one that that fit my vision of what I was becoming continued to cause me constant stress. I was overqualified for many of the available jobs, yet as a new academic, my CV lacked evidence of professional publications that would be an entrée to a fulltime professorship. Those faculty jobs were among the most sought-after. My life was in flux, but it was vital to keep working at anything I could find in or around Albany while building a better relationship with my brother and sister.

This was a period of going through the motions without joy or commitment, waiting for my house on the shore to sell, reducing the price and waiting still more.

Why didn't everyone who saw my dream home fall in love with it the way I had? True, when it rained hard, the garage floor flooded a bit and a puddle formed on the front walk, but it was never more than a half-inch deep.

I signed up for substitute teacher jobs. Subbing meant when the phone rang at five a.m., a loud recorded male voice shouted in the gloom, "You are needed to substitute in the 'Blank Blank' school, in Mr. or Ms. Soand-so's class at 'blank' o'clock. The teacher has left plans on her desk." If the teacher had planned to be out, her plans would be workable. Arriving at the school just after dawn, I'd find the room and quickly figure out what lessons, if any, I'd be teaching.

There were many nightmarish things about subbing, particularly in the special high school which called on substitute teachers frequently. When I met the classes, it was clear why. Those adolescents smelled insecurity and sought to take it to the limit, testing at each turn. The bouncers in the hall were ready to help deal with the kids who were "acting out." Spent and exhausted by 2:30, I'd drive to the nursing home, collapsing next to Mother's bed and try to get her to say something I could understand.

When a full-time sub job as an itinerant speech therapist in the suburbs was offered, I took it. The drive from my apartment to the first elementary school took an hour. In the middle school at dawn, I staggered up several flights where I wrestled a speech therapy schedule around students' already full day. Then I would rush to the high school to occupy a space left by a dearly beloved young speech therapist who died suddenly over the summer. The other Special Ed teachers, stunned by the loss, were less than friendly, seeming barely tolerant of me, this new woman whose presence signaled their grief. I understood it, and I wasn't at my charming best either.

Compared with my long happy career in public school speech therapy, topped off by three years of academic success, my nerves were on edge. Our family's anxiety about mother's worsening condition added to the stress. Sometimes my heart felt like it was doing the twist in my chest.

I found a new doctor and admitted I was having heart palpitations and feeling anxious. They put me through a series of exams, and sent me to specialists. The wait for the results added more to my anxiety. Now I was worried about my physical health. I begged for a referral to see a counselor.

Since my first marriage, whenever I felt depressed, I sought counseling. When my boys were in preschool and I was the director, one of my teachers in the nursery school committed suicide, and I felt myself fighting depression again. Fortunately, I had counseling and a prescription that pulled me out of the doldrums eventually.

While Mother was hooked up to a feeding tube for over a year, counseling was my refuge. The health insurance I inherited from Jim not only enabled me to move from job to job, it also paid for a counselor who taught me how to deal with irrational beliefs. After a while, I learned to judge my own beliefs, realizing that I had some irrational beliefs that were pulling me down. I felt stronger having sorted through them.

Chapter VI Becoming Myself

It is a great gift to become one's own self at last.

Marilyn Zuckerman

Going Home

At the start of the new millennium, my house on the shore finally sold. I was ready to start over and bought a townhouse in the county where I grew up. It had a cathedral ceiling and a loft for my office like the dream house I left in Virginia. In terms of feng shui, it might be considered unfavorable because of its location on a postage-stamp quarter acre at the bottom of a steep hill. However, according to that ancient tradition of believing your environment affects your life, the hill in back of the property provides support for the home. In addition, the house's two stories hold us above the road level in front, and the openness of the cathedral ceiling is tempered by a fan hanging from the slope of the ceiling. Located only five minutes from a major highway to all directions of the compass, it certainly seemed an auspicious location for my new life.

I love the variety of the topography in the Hudson Valley. Settled by the enterprising Dutch in the Colonial Era, the arrival of the railroads and bustling river traffic attracted my English/Scots-Irish ancestry. Driving from one side of the river to the other, my spirits lift with the views across verdant landscape valley to the distant escarpments. I found a renewed appreciation for the small seasonal changes: the bittersweet vines covered with orange berries in the fall; the twinkling Christmas lights strung around the bushes in the winter.

In spring, our garden begins a sequence of blooms starting with pussy willow catkins. The ground where I walk smells familiar on spring mornings after a rain when the worms crawl out on the neighborhood streets. Soon the mats of creeping phlox spread across my small garden, then the lavender bush blooms, attracting white butterflies. In the fall, the brilliant colors of the maples give way to the bareness of winter grays and whites.

In the fall, surrounded by carpets of leaves, I remember my youth when we raked them into great piles to jump into before burning them in the street gutters.

That first year at election time, I wanted to do something to support first lady Hillary Clinton's bid for to become our U.S. senator for New York, long before she ran for president. After hearing her speak at one of her rallies in Albany, I shook her hand and Chelsea's. Afterwards, I contacted the local Democratic Party and volunteered to stuff envelopes. After picking up the envelopes and a yard sign at the campaign office, I started for the door. "Wait," they said, "Here's another one for when the first sign gets stolen." I laughed at the suggestion. Traffic is sparse on our street; I wasn't worried about the possibility and planted the sign in the front yard.

Matt's girlfriend at that time was a reporter for the Associated Press. Speaking with her on the phone the next morning, we were giggling at the possibility someone would take it from my front lawn.

"Is it there?" she asked.

Then I looked out the front window.

"No, it's gone. Who would steal my Hillary sign?"

After some research, she discovered the signs were being sold on eBay for $15. Whatever the reason, it disappeared, so I replaced it with the extra sign. Each evening I removed Hillary's sign from my front lawn, stored it in my garage overnight and proudly replaced it first thing in the morning until Election Day and for weeks afterward. I still have it in my basement, waiting for the day when it will be worth more than $15 on eBay.

Anti-Cinderella

According to a 2004 book called *The Psychology of Women* by Etaugh and Bridges, "A woman doesn't have to have a partner to have a full and satisfying life," That's probably a good thing because there aren't enough men to go around for all of the women after the age of 60. With each year of advancing age, women live longer than men, increasing the ratio of women to men.

The census counted 63 million more women than men in the world. For seniors, the gender disparity was 64 million. Replacing a spouse seems easy for guys. Bob Martin remarried a year after Jean died. Widowers are probably needy as well as lonely. Maybe they don't know how to do the laundry, fry an egg over easy, or dust the furniture. Most men would say they are lucky to live out their old ages in the bosom of wifely care. However, now that I've tasted independence for so long, I'm not inclined to take on that role.

I've noticed that among couples of retirement age, when the husband's health begins to break down, the wives, who are usually younger than their spouses, become hypervigilant, on the lookout for breakdowns in mental or physical capacities. Dealing with falls, memory lapses and driving mishaps reinforces their watchfulness. It looks like extra stress to me, but in addition to love and devotion, perhaps there is an element that satisfies the female need to nurture.

An apocryphal story is told about retirement communities: When a man's wife dies, the women line up on the widower's doorstep with casseroles. In reality, the widowers who remarry tend to choose younger women.

My grandmother was widowed at 34 when my electrician grandfather was electrocuted while repairing a line in a thunderstorm. She was left with three boys to raise as a single woman. My father was the eldest at 11. With the help of an unmarried aunt who lived with them, she went into politics and was elected the Rensselaer city treasurer, serving in that post for 20 years until she retired, still single. Years later, when her sister died, she spent a lot of time taking care of her widower brother-in-law and married him when she was 70. Four years later, she had a stroke and died. Sentimentally, I hope her last years were happy and secure, but I've always felt it was "taking care of Howard" that did her in.

I used to fantasize about finding a real "lapdog," a man who is used to being married, perhaps had several wives already and would like yet another. Maybe he'd be the type to drive me everywhere and wait patiently in the car while I spent his money at Macy's. I know some women find such creatures and I sincerely wish them long and happy lives. However, given their proven frailty, most men don't last as long as their wives, and if they do and their minds stay sound, those couples must feel truly blessed.

Websites springing up on the internet are devoted to the overabundance of the single women. One site, called "Date Hookup," posed the question: "Where are all the 50-60-year-old SINGLE men?" The women complained bitterly, "the older guys who say they wouldn't date a plus-sized woman were actually sitting back on their L-Z-Boys with a beer in one hand and chips in the other, watching football. We are sitting here on a computer and tomorrow is Valentine's Day. We are really looking for that which hardly exists."

To all those who lament their single status, I urge them to give up the Cinderella Complex and, literally, get a life.

It's a relief to not be longing for phone calls looking for Prince Charming or a fair approximation of him at mixers or online. Even though my friends endorsed the idea of my "finding someone," none ever introduced me to any single man they might have known.

If that network couldn't find someone who would be a good match for me, it's not surprising I never found one either. Besides, they knew if I was Jim's "parade," he was my Prince Charming, and it's not reasonable to expect to encounter two in one lifetime, He remains, for me, an irreplaceable partner.

What About Sex?

I hear there is a lot of sexual activity among seniors. Stories of such goings-on in nursing homes might lead one to believe the residents are screwing like bunnies in the spring. When Betty White was asked if she thought seniors had sex, she answered, "If they get a chance, I bet they do."

Here's where I suppose I should explain why for me sex is too much bother. It's also uncomfortable due to the lack of hormones that are essential to a woman's wellbeing earlier in life when finding a husband and having children is primary for most of us. Although the discomfort could be alleviated by hormonal creams and other remedies, I'd eschew them as too much bother, even if I was so inclined. It must be lovely for those seniors who manage to enjoy a partnership that includes sex, but for me, sex became superfluous.

When a guy has to think about ordering a prescription for Viagra and a woman needs to talk to her doctor about a special hormonal cream to be used daily for a month to have intercourse, she has to be highly motivated, which

I'm not. Diana Athill, in her memoir *Somewhere Toward the End* about recovering from the loss of lovers, described it as "gone off the boil." At this point, if you have a male friend or two, why ruin a good relationship with sex?

According to Kegan, sexuality is not essential to a balanced life when one is establishing one's "independent selfhood." Women like me identify with Gloria Steinem who at 80 theorized that a "dwindling libido can be a terrific advantage because brain cells that used to be obsessed are now free for all kinds of great things. Steinem also recalled the old saying, "A woman without a man is like a fish without a bicycle." She continued. "My younger self would have no understanding of that theory, but it makes sense in my mid-70s."

I recall the joke about the man who complained his wife never had an orgasm, to which she replied, "Yes I did, but you weren't in the room."

Colette said, "The end of having lovers was the beginning of an aloneness that is joyous and drenched in sensuality."

I think she meant she would no longer be distracted by the business of being sexual and could concentrate on composing her life as a creative person. After all, happiness means owning your own life, whereas a relationship is a willingly shared ownership.

Truly, single ownership appears a better choice than romance. Having friends who will remain your friends with acceptance of whatever nonsense you get yourself into is something to treasure. I'm lucky to have a few of those in my life.

Advice for Widows

Years after living through it—years when I wasn't ready to get into the dark messy business of dealing with it, I read the books about grief I had shelved earlier. A section in "Finding Your Way After Your Spouse Dies" exhorts the bereaved to "assume control," but then provides a prayer suggesting we leave it to God. According to most books written to comfort the grieving, religion comes in handy. Bible passages are inserted for "reflections" at the end of each bit of advice.

One section suggests reaching out to others, while another advises saying no if you don't feel like going somewhere. In a strangely condescending manner, the author acknowledged that widows are free to have a full and rewarding life without remarrying, choosing to "create your own happiness alone and to take care of yourself." I wonder if widowers would have received the same advice. Skipping through book sections on coping with serious illness and divorce, I found an astute passage about viewing misfortune as a test of character. Indeed, whatever doesn't kill you makes you stronger.

After my cringing period with bumper-car battering, I read *Live Alone and Like It: The Classic Guide for the Single Woman by* Marjorie Hillis. Written semi-seriously way back in 1936, one chapter titled "The Pleasures of a Single Bed" advises the woman alone to appreciate having her own bedroom. Hillis notes the advantage of being able to turn on the lights to read without disturbing a partner. Her advice for the single woman is to "make an art about bedtime rituals" by buying the best bedcovers and "with plenty of pillows and your best nightgown, you could be as seductive in that bed as any other." I am content to sleep in a queen-sized brass bed with two pillows, a warm comforter and a small dog that doesn't care what I'm wearing.

C.S. Lewis wrote *"A Grief Observed"* about his bereavement after the death of his wife. After reading it, I learned he was embarrassed by his own revelations about his raw grief and originally published it under a pseudonym. Remarkably, so many of his friends recommended that book to him, he finally acknowledged it as his own.

Another book urged those suffering sorrow to "concentrate and keep busy at something." It said a busy person doesn't have time to be unhappy. I took the *"busy"* option because I wanted to get back to normalcy, so I shelved the books of comfort and threw myself into studying other things rather than focusing on my widowhood. It reminds me of Kipling's poem, "The Camel's Hump:"

> *The cure for this ill is not to sit still,*
> *Or frowst with a book by the fire,*

But to take a large hoe and a shovel also,
And dig till you gently perspire!

When I went to church, I didn't sit in the congregation praying for comfort. I stayed up front, busy in the choir. Widows like me don't "frowst with a book by the fire."

All the books maintain that guilt is a normal part of grief. Somehow, I sensed that in my case, I couldn't shoulder a mountain of guilt about the manner of Jim's death. I may feel guilty about not taking him to the emergency room with a pain in his neck the night before he died, but neither of us was likely to imagine it would be a harbinger of death at the age of 60. Jim walked for exercise daily, drank red wine each evening and had regular checkups. He had recently seen the doctor for a complete physical prior to his hernia surgery. If guilt is to be placed on anyone for not finding the weak spot in my husband's body, the blame was the doctor's.

One book characterized the dilemmas of a widow having to make decisions that would ordinarily be made by her husband. However, there were no sympathies for a husband who had lost a wife's decision-making skills. Somehow, although I missed Jim constantly, it wasn't because of his telling me what to do. It was for the comfort of his presence, his take on things and his joy in being semi-retired.

Truly, women have come a long way since the 19th century when Horace Greeley combined racism with misogyny, observing, "A widow of doubtful age will marry almost any white man." As one of my brilliant students observed, "Most people believe that feminism is misandry, but it is not." I agree. Widows are no longer desperate to find someone, but to pursue their own dreams.

Encore Woman

For this widow, looking for Mr. Right was wrong. Still looking for my encore career and trying to find my moorings as a single woman in the age of the internet, I threw myself into networking. I created conference presentations and started a business selling colorful story flannel figures for nursery schools, all the while applying for positions at local colleges. One part time position opened and I became part of the great army of adjunct instructors that colleges depend upon these days.

While teaching developmental writing for a local community college, it seemed classes were never long enough to meet the needs of my students. So many of them had overwhelming personal issues; it was hard to focus their attention on correct tense and syntax, while assessing their ability to apply critical thinking skills.

I would have gladly spent time with individual students in the department office, but only a handful took advantage of my offer to meet with them because my assigned office hours were not convenient for them. Their lives were too full and complicated to insert an abundance of learning. Youth appeared to be a condition like an illness to be survived. A young woman student, already pregnant, just returned from the hospital admitting it had been a drug-related emergency visit.

Through my consulting business, I met Deborah Smith, a professor at SUNY Empire State College, a four year college offering online degrees. A good friend and mentor, her knowledge, infectious laugh and creative approach in distance learning courses are truly inspiring. As a creative writer, Deb's travel essays are found anthologies, in Iceland Review, an Icelandic publication, but she also reads them on our local NPR station, WAMC, and recently for 51%, National Productions women's radio program. When she recommended me as an adjunct at the college, my true encore career began.

There is great satisfaction in teaching adult learners. Online classes enable me to spend more time focusing on a student's individual needs for college writing. My new career has three parts. I am the online writing coach, degree program advisor and instructor for online writing classes. My newest challenge is teaching a communication course for the college's international program and a chance to work virtually, enabling me to be face to face on my computer screen with students in the Dominican Republic and Turkey in the same class. We have virtual classes where I can share my desktop like a blackboard for bi monthly meetings related to the online class content. Also, I've created short videos on how to avoid plagiarism and other academic writing topics. All these remain the greatest source of my own lifelong learning

In her 2010 book, *The Third Chapter*, Sara Lawrence Lightfoot's observations of adults after 55 who can "find ways of changing, adapting, exploring, mastering and challenging their energies, skills and passions into new domains of learning" resonates strongly in my present life. Sometimes, I am asked when I will retire. My answer is "Not yet. I'm having too much fun."

Dog Lover

As a young girl walking to the school bus stop, I had to walk through a gauntlet of two big dogs greeting me each morning. First an Irish setter leapt at me; a few steps further, a German shepherd barked menacingly. I wasn't a dog lover; I was a dog fearer.

My husband changed my fear of dogs. We always had a cat, but I never wanted a dog. Jim suggested I look at a litter of Welsh terrier puppies in the home of a colleague who had both the bitch and the sire. It was hard to open myself up to the possibility, but I agreed to look at the puppies.

The apartment door opened on a full-grown terrier— the sire of the litter stood quietly on all fours at my feet, looking up and wagging a stubby tail. I was impressed that he didn't leap at me. The bitch was in the other room with the puppies. They pointed out the runt of the litter, a tiny ball of black and tan with round black eyes and nose to match. My fearful heart melted, and I agreed to adopt her.

For several nights afterwards, I lost sleep because well-meaning people told me, "It's like having a new baby."

"No, I thought, I still have a toddler in diapers. I don't need a new baby."

Nevertheless, we took her home and named her Cookie because she was black and tan like a chocolate chip cookie.

Mornings, it was hard to tell if it was our toddler Chris or Cookie crawling on the floor by our bed since we could see only the tops of their curly black-haired heads. Cookie was a great pal for both our boys as they grew up.

She lived until she was old and stiff and started turning around in the corner. Even now, remembering that little dog mixes pleasure with the pain of loss. I became a dog lover who understood as Anatole France said, "Until one has loved an animal, a part of one's soul remains awakened."

My life with a golden cocker spaniel named Casey began when someone showed me a printout of the dogs in a nearby shelter. His owner was deceased.

My son Matt observed, "as a five-year-old purebred cocker spaniel, in shelter parlance Casey was a 'talented dog,' meaning one that doesn't linger long in shelters—a shelter rock star." He hadn't been there but a day before I whisked him away.

Casey always made me smile—a good dog unless a paper tissue or napkin was within his reach. If you caught him with it early enough, he'd be delighted to return it to you, slightly mashed. Any paper would do. Once I left a $20 bill on a shelf where he could reach it. I found it later in two wadded pieces; the bank took it anyway.

Casey thought people who came to the house were there to play with him. After barking a bit and sniffing their feet, he would offer the visitor a slimy old chewy. When rebuffed, or left alone in the other room, he'd jump up on the couch, hump a pillow and try to bite a corner off. We were silly over him anyway.

One afternoon I took Casey out on his leash and he dragged me across the street to meet a new dog in the neighborhood. This was quite rare. He usually barked to warn me against other dogs. This time, he took one sniff and his stubby tail became a blur. The object of this instant affection was a bedraggled-looking little white toy Maltese/poodle mix. She was being adopted by my neighbor from the Homeward Bound organization that rescued her from neglect and a flea infestation.

When I heard Patty had returned Fluffy the next day, complaining she had a severe allergic reaction to the little thing that wanted to sleep on her bed, I called Homeward Bound right away. Next, they brought her to us in the arms of her foster care volunteer to interview us along with our dog. It appeared they wanted to make sure this adoption would work.

I was allowed to hold Fluffy in an easy chair during the interview as she trembled slightly. Looking on, Casey seemed pleased to see Fluffy in my lap. We passed the interview and were allowed to go to the agency the next day. After filling out a registration form, I signed and initialed four pages of pledges promising to pay all costs of looking after the health and welfare of her seven pounds, Chris and I took her home with us. Later, while holding her in my lap, I sensed her little body relax with what felt like a sigh.

With Fluffy in our household, we go around grinning, and Casey was content to share our attention as he relaxed into his old age, taking long naps on the hearth where, in his deafness, he slept soundly.

Cesar Millan, the dog whisperer, observed "dogs are beneficial to your health. Dogs keep you young in spirit. Give it care, and it gives back."

Loving a dog also inspires poetry. These are about the loves of my life as a dog owner:

Casey, When He Lived with Us

When I see you
There on the hearth
Sitting a little off-center
With stubby tail moving
Or
When I see you
Flail about on the sunny grass

With your feet in the air
Rolling, wallowing in the warm
Like happy dogs do
I say
When I see you,
You too — big curly-haired golden
cocker
Who would never win the best-in-show
I smile again
Through your antics
I smile again.

Casey's Choice

Hey Mom, you know I turn away from
others, but
Let's go over here so I can have a whiff!
Hey Mom,
Can we rescue this one?
This Maltipoo?
Her white coat is scrubby and her body
trembles, but
Oh boy!
She smells so nice!
See my stubby tail blur!

Let's bring her home
To live with us

We'll feed her good; her coat will
flourish.
I'll behave and tolerate everything she
does with ease.
I'll back away from my bowl and let her
have my water.
She's so small, it won't matter when she
jumps on me,
Or pushes through the door first.
She can be my ears and bark so loud,
yours will hurt.
Then I'll know she can warn you, 'cuz I
no longer can.
She might take my chewies away and
store them on your bed,
I won't care; I know you'll love her as
you love me.
When I'm gone, and it might be soon,
Though I never wanted to be there,
She'll warm your lap in the evenings
when I no longer snooze
On the hearth near the fireplace.

In the fall of 2014, Casey's coat turned dull and he had trouble getting up and down from his naps. One day, I caught him staggering against the wall in the midst of a stroke. He was fifteen, ancient for a dog, yet determined to keep on despite his ailing body.

The rain started as I guided Casey out of the car.

He didn't resist as he always had before. "It's time," the vet said, and I knew it, but I also knew I wouldn't be able to control myself when he stopped breathing. Leaving him standing on the table, those still lovely round brown eyes watched me go. I hurried to sit in my car, tears pouring as hard as the rain outside. When the rain cleared a bit, I drove off sniffling. Once home, I sat down and Fluffy came to sit on my lap.

Happiness Is

Joyce Carol Oates said, "I wanted to write a memoir about being a widow. It was going to be the opposite of Joan Didion's. Hers is beautiful and elegiac. Mine would be filled with all sorts of slapstick, demeaning and humiliating things like trash cans whose bottoms are falling out." This resonates with my aftermath of sudden death; it too was sometimes demeaning and slapstick, but that's what makes the tragicomedy of life so interesting.

After reading Oates' memoir, *A Widow's Story,* I can see we had some of the same issues. In the midst of our struggle with grief, we both had to bury a cat. Her cat died on its own, outside in the night, but I had to take mine to the vet and "put her down." Neither of us found it in us to request an autopsy; we both needed to take pills to sleep through the night, and developed a subsequent addiction. During the early stages of grief, we had a common yearning to stay home after accepting dinner invitations and once there, leaving the party first. Oates described developing painful shingles after first getting a negative diagnosis. I complained of heart palpitations and was put through a series of doctor's tests, causing increased anxiety attacks, but no diagnosis. Fortunately, those attacks led to my successful counseling sessions and the opportunity to learn about my own irrational beliefs.

I read a newspaper article titled, "Study contends midlife is miserable." The researcher speculated that perhaps the happiest years of life are the first and the last rather than the middle. I can see that pattern in my own life. In midlife, I was plagued with worry about money, high expectations for my marriage, and the usual concerns of a parent of teenagers. In addition, I went through periods of demanding work assignments that required traveling from one school to another, providing special speech/language services. I yearned to be in one spot, or one school, as a regular staff member. Now that I have that, I enjoy the stimulation of colleagues, sharing projects, writing articles, preparing webinar sessions and serving on committees. I'm the last one to complain about meetings.

In the same vein, I read an article in the New York Times in 2010 that disclosed there may be a biological reason for greater happiness in the mid and later life stages. New brain research shows that "adults in their middle and upper decades seem to have the ability to screen out or tamp down negative emotions." Between the ages of 50 and 65, or beyond can be the most transformative time of our lives. Erik Erikson talked about this stage of life as the penultimate stage; it can be characterized by a crisis like mine. Married or single, this generative stage is the opportunity to leave a legacy, to mentor and to move forward to a realization of one's life purpose.

Indeed, given a fair amount of health and economic security, older people find a renewal of life and along with it, sometimes, love. I agree with the renewal part, but I don't need romantic love to breathe. I prefer the air of freedom now; somehow, I think I'm better at relationships because I don't expect a lot from them.

Yes, Charles Schulz, "Happiness is a warm puppy," and my little dog is a constant source of joy, but happiness is found in a myriad other ways too, when one is starts to realize it.

Happiness is having enough lucre to spend on personal maintenance like pedicures and trips to Ann's hair salon. Either one is a fine cure for a burgeoning headache.

Happiness is going to the orchard market in the fall with my sons who help carry the heavy bundles of apples, pears, squash, while quaffing cider and eating a cider donut. Afterwards, making applesauce fills the house with a homey scent.

Happiness is being published. At this point, it is better than sex. Seeing something I wrote published in the local newspaper was as thrilling as it was to receive a published copy of my Doctoral dissertation. In March of

2010, my essay for Women's History Month was published in Sunday's *Albany Times Union* along with the online version featuring pictures. I was becoming a local Women's History month media queen when the next year; I recorded another personal essay for our local NPR station also appeared in the paper. I was happily invited to read personal and travel essays with a group of other writers at our local Arts Center. Somehow, I didn't mind the hard work and the results were satisfying. Also, it was joyous to find my articles in academic journals after a long period of reviewing the literature prior to writing.

Happiness is life-long learning that comes with expanding my circle of academic colleagues and planning to research important technological issues of online instructor feedback. My new mission is to help other instructors discover the fun of using 21st Century feedback tools with their online students.

Happiness is having friends with similar musical interests. Summers where I live now are full of wonderful choices: Opera at Bard college or Saratoga: ballet or the Philadelphia Symphony at Saratoga Performing Arts Center; Glimmerglass Performances an hour away, and Tanglewood, with its broad lawns and Boston Symphony performances enchanting to enjoy with close friends or family.

Happiness is having significant work to do. For me, it is online teaching and mentoring. Distance learning provides a vehicle where I can be more thoughtful and understanding than under the pressure of the fifty-minute face-to-face class. Sitting in front of the computer early in the morning with sun streaming in my large study windows, birds flit among the sumacs; the house is quiet and I am teaching asynchronously. My adult online students have left questions, discussion postings, and assignments that await my feedback. I praise their efforts and write gentle directions on how to strengthen their writing skills.

Happiness is teaching with Internet tools—meeting online with a class of students from separate continents; their computer cameras enable face-to-face discussions with me while I use my desktop as a teaching blackboard. My students' end-of-term evaluations are often a benediction for my efforts and sometimes, amusing. Recently, one wrote: "Professor Russell *is* a teacher by nature—she has to be. I've learned so much from her, and in my opinion, she should set the standard for online college professors...or else she should be paid twice as much. Possibly three times."

Happiness is having sons who make me laugh along with the company of friends with the same interests— friends who are busy and productive, but who enjoy concerts, plays, trips to the opera and making travel plans. I am blessed with friends I can call to share experiences and offer help when needed. Friends can offer advice, but it's lovely knowing I don't necessarily have to take it.

Sometimes happiness is finding a Bill Bryson book I have yet to read.

After a decade of widowhood, time is slipping away, taking a portion of former muscle flexibility and youthful skin with it. My sons are still bachelors and I have no grandchildren. My stepchildren and their families are far away on the other side of the continent and Florida. But these things no longer matter because—inexplicably—I feel happier in this *Generative* stage of later adulthood than when I was married and in my 40's. The reason? I think it is because my happiness no longer depends upon others. It's a hard-won prize, and I treasure it.

I have emerged stronger and dared to say I am happy, tempting fate even further by declaring, "I'm doing so well, and am so happy with my life, nothing can get me down." What folly to tempt fate that way! Crass optimism? The glass may be half full, but there is that other half where health and family concerns reside.

Facing the Inevitable

It was becoming time to release his remains from the shelf, and time to purchase a couple of plots for both of our cremated remains in a cemetery. Still, I struggled to accept the idea of cremation for myself. Why was it so easy for Jim? He always spoke about his ashes without using the word cremation. The idea still repulses me, but so does the alternative—slow decomposition. I suppose it's best not to take up too much space in the earth with expensive hardware and full body remains. I could be that disposable item too, and through the march of days since Jim's passing, my time gets closer.

I called my sister, the family's keeper of records, and genealogist. "Suz, I think I'm about to buy a place for Jim's ashes and myself for when the time comes."

"Oakwood Cemetery in Troy is a good place," she suggested, "We have relatives there."

"Yes, I know." I took my newly widowed friend, Novalyn, whom everyone called Novi, to the crematorium for a chamber music concert. It was performed in a small chapel in the building amid stained glass windows and stone carvings. Afterward, we took a little tour and saw where they placed the bodies to be consumed by fire. Novi went along with me, clearly not at all inspired or comforted. I asked her if she and John had spoken about final arrangements prior to his death.

She said no, they hadn't because they were too busy fighting cancer for his life. Novi died a couple of years ago, so that was our last visit together. I could tell she didn't appreciate my prying question. Our friendship was stymied after that—a friendship lasting from the time we were roommates in grad school and the births of our two children, each within six months of the other.

Novi, I'm sorry. I promise if you could come to my house again. I would not bring you to another cemetery. I know you handled the whole dispersing ashes thing by taking your son and daughter to the dock on Long Island sound where they scattered John's ashes out in the water.

But I still have some of Jim's left, and I need to find the right place for that mahogany box with the rest of Jim's remains inside.

Finding the final place: Does one shop around? Comparison shop for the best buy? A place on a hillside? On top of the hill? Perhaps under a tree? Is there a stream nearby? Does it matter? Shall I choose based on price? How much for a cremation plot or a section? The most inexpensive plots cost $800 for each single space. Now I could afford it. How about having another ceremony? A graveside ceremony? Let's not think about that now, Scarlett. Let's just decide where to go.

Suzanne reminded me, "Mom and Dad; Uncle Howard and Aunt Vera are in Albany Rural Cemetery. They bought their plots 20 years before they needed them."

"Yes, and I remember they have a nice cremation burial section as well."

Albany Rural Cemetery, the resting place of 55 Albany mayors, five governors, 34 members of Congress, 8 presidential cabinet members and one president—Chester Arthur. It's only 11 minutes and 2.8 miles away —down the hill to the river, across the bridge, up the Menands hill, turn right, drive in. The first place to stop is the Linden Grove Cremation Garden designated for cremated remains. There are no upright gravestones there, only sturdy stone plaques on the ground with a name and life dates marked on each.

Sorry Jim, I did what you wanted. Some of your ashes went in the Lincoln Center fountain, but how could you have known there would be more in your big box? The remaining remains still need a final—truly final place for you—and yes, me as well.

Maybe a few ghosts will return—the young couple floating in pajamas, said to be sighted over the years; Chester Arthur could come by to say hello and talk politics. Maybe there will be one of those glowing orbs someone said they saw. You might enjoy that.

On the phone with Bobbi on my weekly call to her in Florida: "I think I'm going get a plot for Jim and me. Finally take his remains out of my bedroom closet. A plot for the two of us."

"Good, you can't keep him in the closet forever. Poor Chris, what would he do with both of you in the closet?"

The thought of two of us on the shelf—mournful containers, side by side in the closet, or maybe my new fancy urn added to Jim's masculine mahogany box— suddenly struck me as very funny—now I'm almost falling out of my chair laughing as tears fill my eyes.

"You told me once you'd never have another relationship if you kept him there in your closet."

Wiping my eyes from the laughter, "That's only Feng Shui nonsense. I don't really believe it has a shred of effect on my life, although I must admit I'm very diligent about throwing out dead cut flowers as soon as they start to fade in a vase. When I open the closet, looking for my out-of-season sweaters or socks, the box is on the top shelf in a wicker basket where it fits perfectly."

"Yes, but you must think about it being there." "I don't, and I hardly ever look at our pictures on the wall in my bedroom.

When I do stop to look at the photos while hunting for something in the dresser, I admire Jim's sweet brown eyes, his high forehead topped with the curly gray hair and the glasses he wore then. I'm wearing the gold chain necklace he gave me. We are both smiling as if we just shared a joke.

These are only fleeting thoughts now, thoughts that vanish quickly. Life is still moving forward with my head full of the day's possibilities, expectations, necessities and occupations.

Was there something wrong with my unsentimental view of the past? I see both sides—the masks of comedy and tragedy. Should I take on the tragic face? No, it's no longer time to mourn. It's time to laugh at the inevitable tragedy of life and live it while you've got it. Humor takes the sting out of loss, overcomes it, makes it a more agreeable companion.

After several weeks of rain and gray skies, a sunny Friday is probably a big help when you plan to buy your own burial plot. Albany Rural Cemetery is still active despite the city's growth around it. A fountain plays on a central pond and stately old trees provide shade and greenery. Most of the monuments are in excellent condition. It's a lovely spot to spend eternity. Sheltered by linden trees, the Linden Grove Cremation Garden will have our remains side by side, moldering under engraved stone plaques, only a ten-minute drive across the river.

"Patient appeared stiffly controlled." my doctor wrote in my health file from my last physical exam after Jim died. Yes, I did struggle to hold myself together then. I found myself in the same frame after deciding to buy the plots, on my own, telling myself it's simply a matter of greeting the nice clerk I spoke with on the phone, and selecting two plots in the Linden Grove section.

I found the cemetery office in the old pink sandstone cemetery building; after initial greetings, and discussing available plots with "Kind John," the cemetery clerk, I chose plots 15 and 16, still fighting hard to keep my emotions level, not giving in to the hard tug, but feeling a gathering sensation inside.

Kind John excused himself to prepare my documents in the next room. The stone walls reverberated with clacking sounds. "Do I hear a typewriter?" I said, keeping my tone light.

"Yes," he said, "It's a manual. Nothing changes around here, but our customers don't seem to mind." His small attempt at humor worked, smoothing out the ball in my stomach. With the plot documents in hand, there were further questions for another form: "His first name? (James). Middle? (Robert). Tears pushed to the fore as I said his middle name, knowing I was the only one outside of his sons who knew it. Last? (Russell). Where was he born? (Ithaca). *Wrong, he moved to Ithaca with his mother from Williamsport. Pa., where his father lived.*

This was getting burdensome. His mother's name? (Ruth). His father's? (James). His birthdate? (August 4, 1932). Date of death? (January 22, 1993). "OK," he said gently, handing me the documents. "Please check to make sure this information is correct and call me." I agreed, unprepared for the final salvo: "When you decide on the interment date, please bring the certificate from the funeral home that arranged the cremation." Certificate? Where could it be? Flustered again, I couldn't remember ever seeing it. Kind John reassured me they would call the funeral home to get a copy. Relieved, I left for home to search for documentation.

I gratefully took the opportunity to check my answers with the documents I had at home, still feeling inadequate and befuddled. Along with the death certificate came fine memories, vivid photos and memorial programs. I took the box/urn from the shelf and extracted it from the wicker basket where it had gathered a thin layer of dust. Turning over the heavy box, I noticed a small metal plaque on the bottom, that read:

200 PLUS
By Frederick Town Urn Company
PO Box 2171
Winchester, VA
Call: 703-662-1958 or 1-800 722-1958

Jim, at six foot two, flirted with 200 plus pounds for years, but it looked good on him. Now I knew why he was in a box and not an urn. He was too big for an urn, and still too big and heavy in the box labeled 200 PLUS. His 200 pounds concentrated in a box, now he'd be in his final spot under the linden trees, near me now and when it's my turn, our children and his grandchildren will be able to visit us both in years to come.

Decision made, I ended that sunny, eventful day meeting with my neighbor Rosario, a newer widow who shares our side by side townhouse roof. We agreed to contract with the lowest bidder for a fine new roof. We widows will be our own protection.

Randi's Story

Matt was working in New York City for six months in the spring after the destruction of hurricane Sandy. He came home for a weekend in March. At brunch with me and Chris, he announced: "I have something to tell you that I've known for a couple of months, but I wanted to tell you in person."

Yikes, he's 49, was he finally getting married? No.

He showed me a Binghamton newspaper clipping from 1960 with pictures of the cast of the Binghamton Opera's production of *Die Fledermaus*. It identified Jim Russell as singing the role of the jailor. Matt pointed to the picture of one of the women, "Do you recognize the soprano?"

"I remember that name and I've seen this clipping before," I said. "Jim mentioned her once as he recalled singing with the Binghamton Opera. I seem to remember there was something mysterious about how she left and I think he didn't know why or where she went."

Matt continued, "Not only was she the lead in the opera company, she was Ed's first grade teacher before Dad and Ed's mother separated. Evidently, she and Dad dated during the run of the opera, and after a short while, she discovered she was pregnant. Without telling Dad about the pregnancy, she left her teaching job and moved to New York City."

After the baby girl was born in the Lying in Hospital, she was placed with an adoption agency that exclusively placed babies with Jewish families.

What would motivate a woman to deliver a baby without telling the father? Maybe because he wasn't Jewish or perhaps she never wanted to have children.

Being a single mother wasn't easy in those days and the father already had a young son. Certainly, she wouldn't have been able to concentrate on her career, which subsequently became quite successful in the 60's and 70's in music publishing and producing shows from her office on Broadway.

The child grew up as Randi Solomon, the adopted daughter of a loving Jewish family in the city. When her adoptive mother died, she wanted to know about her birth mother and father. Her family had a vague idea that her birth mother's last name began with "P." Armed with that information and her birthdate, she searched the birth records in the New York City Public library and confirmed her birth mother's name. Resolving to meet the woman, she contacted the adoptive agency. Their records described the father as athletic, a teacher, and an opera singer, but not his name. However, with her birth mother's name, it wasn't hard to find that she was still living in New York. Randi called her and they agreed to meet in a restaurant.

Instead of a joyous scene with the 40-year-old daughter meeting the unmarried, childless mother after so many years, it wasn't. The woman was accompanied by a friend and quite guarded. The woman was suspicious of Randi's motives, but she did mention other relatives, an aunt and a cousin living in another state. When they parted, she said, "Call me again, but not every day." Despite this cold parting, at least, Randi learned her father's name was Jim Russell.

In addition to her birth father's name, she learned the names and locations of her cousins and aunts. Hoping for a friendlier reception, she called a cousin for a chat; this prompted a call from her birth mother.

"What are you trying to do? Stay away from my family. Don't try it again." She told Randi to "consider herself lucky" she was willing to meet her at all.

Reeling from the rebuff, Randi slid into depression. She still had her adoptive father, but now, in addition to grieving for the woman who raised her, she was rejected by her birth mother again. Interestingly, their careers were similar. Randi became a music director, with success in composing and marketing jingles and other commercial recordings. Her music accompanies the outdoor Christmas shows at the Venetian in Las Vegas. Her birth mother had a successful career producing Broadway shows.

Ten years later, 9/11 happened, and Randi's reaction to the enormous loss of life propelled her to hire an investigative genealogist who had her own TV show and was featured on Oprah's. The investigator learned that Jim Russell had died, but had two sons in New York. She hoped to find a warmer reception with her birth father's family. When the investigator called Matt's number to ask if he would mind hearing from Randi; he quickly agreed.

Since Randi was back in the city to be with her aging father at the time Matt was working there, she summoned the courage to call him. They spoke and arranged to meet the next day at his midtown hotel. When Matt saw her, he knew immediately she was his sister. Incredibly, they were dressed the same – black leather jacket, jeans and a baseball cap. Matt realized she was gay. "It's as if Dad was reincarnated as a lesbian," he said. Randi was living with her partner, now wife, Barbara, in Florida.

Matt consented to have a DNA test, but it wasn't necessary. She looked so much like his father and his younger brother Chris: curly dark hair, brown eyes and chiseled nose, the same handsome features but more delicate.

One by one, we met Randi, immediately feeling a closeness, a true kinship not only fostered by her uncanny resemblance to Jim, but also by her sincere desire to know us and, by proxy, become acquainted with her father. She easily told us her story.

In the process of sharing photos with Randi, we retrieved the best of Jim as a father and husband. Chris gathered all our pictures of him and many of Jim's mother, and some of his birth father, also named James, who played football with the Philadelphia Eagles when Jim was born. He made copies and sent them to her. One photo, shows a long-forgotten visit to the Cloisters overlooking the Hudson on a blustery blue sky day, I'm wearing my red coat and matching head scarf fastened tightly against the wind. I'm clutching Jim in his pea coat, both of us grinning from ear to ear. In another photo, he obviously had just told a funny story; next to him, head tilted upwards, I wear an expression of delighted love. Another favorite photo is of Jim with a silly smile holding a goat in front of a small truck with the name "Jim Russell" printed on the side in bold letters.

Randi's genealogical searches of her father's origins provided previously unknown facts about Jim's lineage. His sons learned about their father's family in western Pennsylvania and his grandmother's origins in Michigan. Among 17 generations of ancestors from England were a significant number of bishops, an archbishop and notably Sir Maurice Abbot, who was Lord Mayor of London in 1638.

Jim wanted a daughter during both of my pregnancies. He already had a fine son in California, where Ed and his mother moved after she and Jim were divorced. We picked out a name for a daughter; she would be Ruth, since both Jim's mother and mine were named Ruth. But first came Matt, and 15 months later, Chris. What would he have thought, if he knew about his daughter? It's hard to speculate, knowing the pain separation from Ed caused him. Nevertheless, a wonderful piece of him had come into our lives, to love and cherish. At last, a daughter, and she is his.

One of the last times time I was in Florida with Bobbi, Randi drove to meet us at a restaurant in St. Augustine. Coming through the restaurant door with the bright sun behind her, a tall dark silhouette, shifting her weight carefully from one leg to the other, she moved precisely as her father moved the first night he walked by me. Randi asked me if it was love at first sight. Oh yes, it was, and her presence was heightening my memory of him. When she asked, "What would he say if I walked in the door?" I said I think he would say, "Would you like a drink?"

Next spring, all of Jim's children Ed, Matt, Chris and Randi will gather with me at the Linden Grove Cremation Garden plots in Albany Rural Cemetery. At last, I will take his heavy mahogany box down from the shelf and carry it in the wicker basket to our final resting place. We will bring guitars, sing, cry a bit, read some poetry and say a prayer while laying Jim's ashes to rest at last.

Now that I'm old enough to know better, I'm off the bumper cars; I have joyful work, and my sons, including two step-children, love me and I love them. I am contented to sleep alone with my affectionate little dog. As Jim wrote to his friends the Christmas before his sudden death, "Life is sweet."

Epilogue From the Shore of Kiwassa Lake In the Adirondacks

The last time I raced my sunfish,
You rigged the sail and pushed me
into deeper water,
Smiling, waving goodbye from the shore,
You knew
I must run my race alone,
Winning today; losing tomorrow,
Taking your tacit blessing with me.

Miriam S. Russell

225

About the Author

Miriam S. Russell

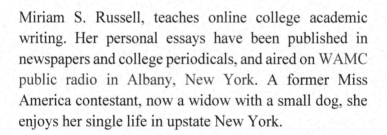

Miriam S. Russell, teaches online college academic writing. Her personal essays have been published in newspapers and college periodicals, and aired on WAMC public radio in Albany, New York. A former Miss America contestant, now a widow with a small dog, she enjoys her single life in upstate New York.